Amy Julia Becker gets to the heart of our most valuable moments with our children—the ones in which we laugh, cry, and marvel at the unexpected revelation of truth and joy in our everyday lives. *Small Talk* reveals how talking with our children about the most important things in life actually ends up growing *us* up just as much, if not more, than them.

—GABE AND REBEKAH LYONS, cofounders of Q and authors of *The Next Christians* and *Freefall to Fly*, respectively

Small Talk is a gift to parents who long to connect with their children about the joys and everyday rituals that sustain us, as well as about the griefs that capsize our hearts. Amy Julia Becker is an astute observer; she watches and names how, along with her children, she is maturing and coming to understand the world and her place in it. Thoughtful, wise, and engaging, Becker's work inspires me to live with intention and keep alert to the presence of God. Highly recommended.

—JENNIFER GRANT, author of *Love You More*, *MOMumental*, *Disquiet Time*, and *Wholehearted Living*

One reason, among many, that Amy Julia Becker is a great writer is that she pays attention. Her reflections in *Small Talk* will inspire you to pay attention to the small wise voices in your world as well.

—MARGOT STARBUCK, author of *Not Who I Imagined*

Amy Julia Becker does big things in *Small Talk*, delighting and challenging readers with stories of conversations with her kids—and the thoughts on life, love, and God that follow. *Small Talk* is a must-read for anyone who's ever learned about the bigness of life from the smallest of folks—or anyone who wants to.

—CARYN RIVADENEIRA, author of *Broke: What Financial Desperation Revealed about God's Abundance* and producer and host of Midday Connection on Moody Radio

Amy Julia tells stories of life with children in graceful prose that is rich in theological insight. Parents will find themselves nodding in empathetic recognition as they read her accounts of the joys and challenges of family life, but *Small Talk* is by no means a book for parents only. This is much more than a book about life with kids; it is a book about life's most complex questions.

—RACHEL MARIE STONE, author of *Eat with Joy:*
Redeeming God's Gift of Food

Small Talk goes far beyond trite observations that our children teach us patience or rekindle wonder. Amy Julia Becker offers readers a nuanced exploration of how loving her children through significant moments and hard questions has stretched and deepened her own understanding of what matters most and why. *Small Talk* offers wisdom that even the cynical and the exhausted can grab on to as we go about this bewildering business of raising children.

—ELLEN PAINTER DOLLAR, author of *No Easy Choice: A Story of*
Disability, Parenthood, and Faith in an Age of Advanced Reproduction

Small Talk made me want to suspend time in the moments with my children that I'm so often tempted to brush past. But more, Amy Julia's narrative doesn't just allure us into finding God and His fingerprints in these moments in the lives of our children; she calls us to a place of seeking God tucked away in *all* of life's seemingly simple minutes.

—SARA HAGERTY, author of *Every Bitter Thing Is Sweet*

Through story after beautiful story, Amy Julia demonstrates all the extraordinary ways God reveals his amazing grace to us through our children. She also reveals the profound beauty that can radiate through a parent's willingness to be authentic about their own vulnerability, weakness, and need. Amy Julia has the gift of reminding me that truly, "All is grace."

—JEANNIE CUNNION, author of *Parenting the Wholehearted Child*

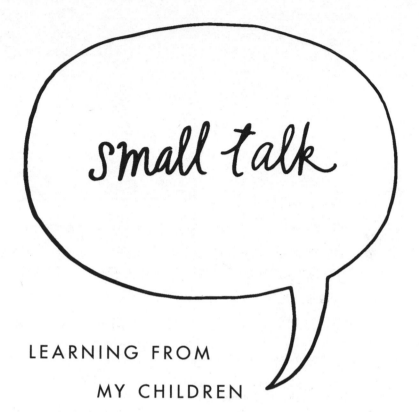

small talk

LEARNING FROM
MY CHILDREN
ABOUT WHAT MATTERS MOST

amy julia becker

ZONDERVAN®

For Peter, with thanks

I'm writing this in part to tell you that if you ever wonder what you've done in your life, and everyone does wonder sooner or later, you have been God's grace to me, a miracle, something more than a miracle.

—MARILYNNE ROBINSON, *GILEAD*

contents

PART THREE
growing up

beginning

It snowed yesterday. The view outside the kitchen window is idyllic — trees hand-painted with delicate white strokes, sunshine glinting off the crystal expanse, a landscape of comforting beauty.

The scene inside my heart isn't nearly as lovely. Our oldest child, Penny, has been home sick from school for two days, and her illness came on the heels of a long weekend. The younger two — William, age five, and Marilee, about to turn three — were sent home from school early yesterday, and today they have a delayed opening because of the snow.

It is too cold to go sledding. I have never been one for arts and crafts. I want to park all three of them in front of three separate screens and pour a cup of tea and count the hours until they return to activities directed by adults other than me.

But at breakfast, Penny says, "Mom, can we do family devotions?" Marilee's eyes get big with anticipation as she claps and agrees. "Famwy bevotions!" William pulls the bin of musical instruments to the center of the playroom floor.

We've been having "family devotions" for a few months now, and the title of this event suggests more piety than the actual experience deserves. Last week, Marilee got out a broken bongo and "played" it with a candle until we realized wax was flying all over the room. William prefers to pick up a recorder and whistle shrilly in my ear. We often have to take away Penny's book as she tries to read on her own instead of paying attention to the one-minute Bible lesson. All three wriggle through the prayer time. They fight over which song comes next.

But we keep trying.

So on this snowy morning, I sit cross-legged on the floor, guitar on my lap, with the kids scattered around the room. I clunk my way through the chords for "Holy, Holy, Holy" and smile at Marilee's three-year-old voice struggling to form the archaic words of the old hymn.

It comes time to pray and Penny says, "Wow God for loving me." William spends most of the time working on a Lego castle until we pray for what we need. "I need Nana Nana and Geeka to feel better," he says. Every time we gather like this, William prays for my aging grandparents, and every time I am struck by how easily I forget others in need, how my own prayers so often neglect the ones I love.

Even without my husband, Peter, who has already left for work, even though I am harried by the snow days and the sick days and the long weekend, it is a sweet time. I am grateful, feeling as though I have received a spiritual booster shot that might just get me through a few days of chores and to-do lists and piano practice and ballet class and trying to keep everyone occupied without immediately resorting to electronic devices.

Then I notice the time. We've had two extra hours to get ready, and we're still going to be late for school. I put the guitar away without letting Marilee perform her customary ritual of latching it in place. I remove the song binder from Penny's hands with more force than necessary. I speak in a stern voice: "Socks. Boots. Backpacks."

They head out the door, and I run back to the kitchen for my phone. I come outside to find Penny, nose running, tears streaming, gazing plaintively at William, who sits inside the minivan, arms crossed over his body, seat belt on.

"Mom!" Penny turns to me. "William won't let me sit in the special seat."

William stares straight ahead. His eyes are as cold as the air outside.

"Pen, you know it's his turn. Go ahead and get in the car."

I buckle Marilee and hoist myself into the front seat.

Soon Penny is wailing. "William hit me! He hit me!"

My torso seems to be expanding, as if a flame has just sparked inside and the tinder has begun to crackle. It is probably true that William hit her, though I doubt he inflicted any harm. My anger right now is directed toward Penny, my oldest, the one who should have learned by now to obey me and ignore her little brother's taunts.

"Penny," I say, and then I use a word my children rarely hear me utter. "You can stay home alone or you can get in your seat." It is an empty threat, but she doesn't call my bluff.

She whimpers and takes her place.

I exhale an angry sigh, followed by another expletive, and listen for the click that signals she is secure.

As we back out of the garage, Marilee asks, "You aw done yewwing now?"

Her little voice cuts through my smoldering emotion. I stop the car in the middle of the driveway and say, "Okay everybody, I think it's time for all of us to say sorry for being jerks."

"You was a jerk, Mommy?" Marilee asks.

"Yep. I was a jerk for yelling at Penny and Penny was a jerk for crying about the backseat and William was a jerk for the way he treated Penny."

We pull out into the street and I say, "Do we want to be lovers or jerks?"

"I want to be a lover!" Penny yells.

William is still staring straight ahead, but his face is softer than it was a few minutes before. After a long pause, he says, "Mom, I want to be a lover. But I also want the special seat."

I catch his eye in the rearview mirror. I think he's trying to hold back a smile.

"Here's the thing, everybody," I say. "God loves us even when we are jerks. And God forgives us even when we are jerks. And God gives us the power to learn how to love instead of being jerks. That's what I want. I want to love you more and more and be a jerk less and less."

They nod. Penny wipes away her tears. We drive to school.

It is the pattern of our life together. In the midst of snow days and sickness, in the midst of yelling and tears, grace enters in.

This book is a series of reflections from my past few years of parenting, beginning when I was pregnant with Marilee and moving in a rough chronological order through my children's young lives. It is not a how-to guide. It is not filled with advice. It is, I hope, a word of encouragement that good things can emerge out of the hard but ordinary everyday moments. It is, I hope, a reminder that on those days when you wonder if there is any meaning in the dishes and disputes and diapers, you are not alone. It is also, I suppose, an exhortation to pay attention—to the words and thoughts and actions of these little ones we so easily overlook.

For a long time, I thought my children were a distraction from the work God was doing in my life and in the world around me. I am starting to realize they *are* the work God is doing in my life. They are the invitation to give, to receive, to be humbled, to grow. They are the vehicles of grace.

PART ONE

holding on

Love is what carries you,
for it is always there,
even in the dark, or most in the dark,
but shining out at times like gold stitches
in a piece of embroidery.

—WENDELL BERRY, *HANNAH COULTER*

birth

As a newborn baby breathes and cries, so the signs of
life in a newborn Christian are faith and repentance,
inhaling the love of God and exhaling an initial cry of
distress. And at that point what God provides, exactly
as for a newborn infant, is the comfort, protection,
and nurturing promise of a mother.

—N.T. WRIGHT, *SIMPLY CHRISTIAN*

I am sitting on the white tiled floor, my back against the wall,
hugging my knees to my belly, which is just beginning to expand
with new life. Penny, age four, faces me from her perch on the
potty. I study her face—the eyes that always look so earnest,
the round cheeks, the full pink lips. I need to cut her bangs. They
are in danger of getting tangled in her long eyelashes.

"Tell me a story about when I's born," she says. Her glasses
sit low on her nose, and she looks like an attentive librarian,
eager to hear whatever I have to offer.

I make a noise that is the combination of a smile and a
sigh. It is a story I love. It is also a story I have told many times
before. The recent announcement of this new brother or sister
has piqued her interest, so I am recounting these details for the
fourth time in a matter of days.

The baby inside shifts a little bit, as if she, too, has perked up for the words to come. Penny puts her elbows on her knees, her chin in her hand.

"Well, when you were born it was wintertime. Just a few days after Christmas. And I woke up in the middle of the night because my tummy felt kind of funny. I read a book for a while, and my tummy still felt funny, and finally I woke up your dad. I told him I thought you were coming."

Her eyes get even wider, and a smile spreads across her face. "And then you got the nursery ready?"

"Yep. We spent the next three hours hanging pictures on your walls and washing clothes to get things ready for you to come home. And finally I went to the hospital, and the doctor checked and she said—"

Penny interrupts. "I can feel your baby's head!" She opens up her palms, as if she is the doctor expressing wonder and incredulity.

"That's right. So we called your Nana and your aunts and they started driving to the hospital. And your dad went home to get my clothes and some pillows and things like that. And it hurt and hurt and hurt and then I got some medicine and it felt a lot better."

Penny nods, those big eyes now more sympathetic than excited.

"And then it was time to push. And I pushed and I pushed—"

"And I shot into the world! Who catched me?"

I laugh. "Your dad and your Nana were there, but the doctor caught you. And then I held you in my arms and we were so happy because we had you. Our beautiful baby girl."

She nods again. She is familiar with these words. She thinks we have come to the end.

But this time, for the first time, I continue.

"But, Pen," I say, "after you were born, I was scared. Because the doctors told us you had Down syndrome."

She looks at me as though I have slapped her. Hard. It is a look of shock and confusion, and I want to pull my words back. But to pull them back would mean returning to that woman four years earlier and convincing her there is nothing to fear.

Penny says in a quiet voice, "Why you were scared?"

My own voice catches as I tell her. "I was scared because I thought Down syndrome would hurt you." I think back to those initial moments. How much I didn't want to believe it. How I ached when I saw the pain in Peter's eyes. I realize the answer I have given her is only partially true. "And I was scared it would hurt us."

"Oh." She blinks her eyes the way she does when she's thinking hard. She struggles a little to pull up her underwear, flushes the toilet, and turns to face me.

"But, sweetie," I say, pushing my weight off the floor and resting my hand on her shoulder. "It didn't hurt you. And it didn't hurt us. So we didn't need to be scared anymore."

"So then you were happy?"

The story feels so complicated to me, and yet she has stated the simple reality. We were scared. And then we were happy. And now we are happy, because we have her.

I reach out my arms and pull her close. Her face rests on my belly, and I think about welcoming this little one who will join us in a few months' time as I say, "We are so happy, every day, to have you in our lives."

* * *

William's birth story is as familiar to my children as Penny's. Both of them could recite the details: I went into labor in the summertime. Penny stayed with my mother while Peter drove me to the hospital. On the way, we had to pull over so I could vomit on the side of the road. William's head was so big the doctor had to use a vacuum to pull him out.

But I rarely dwell on the difficulty of that labor. The kids laugh when they hear about the vomit, and I don't tell them I couldn't stand up and didn't want anyone to visit because I was too wiped out the first day after he was born. I never mention the look of concern on Peter's face when I didn't have the strength to hold our new baby. Those details don't stay with me as much as the feeling of serenity the next day, when I was able to waddle around without feeling faint, when I gazed out of our picture window over Long Island Sound and my heart felt as peaceful as the quiet water.

Even before I told Penny more of her story, I regretted the contrast between my thoughts about her birth—my memories of hurt and fear, the feeling that I was drowning and might never come up for air—and the narrative I have created to talk about her brother's entrance into the world. I suppose I wished I could redo Penny's birth and make it into its own Hallmark card, with a mother who already understood that each life we are given comes out beautiful and broken, that every human being who enters the world does so with neediness, vulnerability, limitations, and gifts.

But recently I have started to wonder if my memory of Penny's birth—the joy and pain and fear and love all mixed together—holds the more appropriate emotional narrative for the birth of each of my children. Perhaps Penny's story is the only one I tell with accuracy. The only one that hints at the years of both pain and wonder to come.

As I've told my children stories of easy, peaceful, happy births, I've thought more about the way I talk about spiritual birth. I have a story of spiritual birth that I can offer in simple terms. I could say it happened at my baptism, that God welcomed me as an infant and I've been part of the family ever since. Or I could say it happened in high school, when I experienced for the first time a yearning and a need for something or someone greater than me. I could tell stories of answered prayer and personal transformation since then. Or I could tell the real story, the one that involves both faith and faithlessness, unanswered prayer and unexpected grace, doubt and love, sorrow and sinfulness and anger and pain and hope and joy and gratitude too.

Just as physical birth is messy and complicated, being born spiritually is not a neat and tidy transformation. It is an ongoing story of neediness and growth and trust.

As I begin to prepare our household for this third child — finding the bassinet and infant car seat, dusting off Penny's newborn clothes, searching bins in the basement for rattles and swaddling blankets and teething rings — I begin to remember the vulnerability of new life. New babies have to learn even the simplest things — how to eat and sleep and smile. Now that I've gone through infancy with the older two, I understand that birth is only the beginning of a relationship that asks a lot of the parent and expects nothing but dependency from the child. Maybe dependency is all God asks of us.

I think about Jesus' words to the religious teacher Nicodemus in the gospel of John, his insistence that to know God we must be "born again." I wonder if I have always oversimplified that overused phrase. The biblical writers do describe new birth as redemption, becoming as white as snow in an instant. But I also assume Jesus knew what birth was like—bloody and painful and risky in the midst of the blessing of it all. So perhaps Jesus was telling Nicodemus that entering into God's family involves neediness and ignorance and constant attention. It's exhilarating and irrevocable and hard and messy and slow and immediate, all at the same time.

Penny's birth provoked everything I could feel, from delight to despair. And as God's Spirit grows me up, calling forth the best in me and helping me see the worst for what it is, I realize that this new spiritual life is just as painful, and just as glorious, as entering into this world to begin with.

* * *

After that moment in the bathroom, Penny keeps asking for this new version of her birth story. Again and again, when I tell her about our fear when we found out she had Down syndrome, she receives the story and repeats it back to me.

But one day we are driving together, just the two of us, and I get to this now familiar ending. She interrupts. "Mom, stop. Don't tell the Down syndrome part."

My lungs seem to squeeze my heart, as if my fist has gotten lodged behind my sternum.

"Why not, sweetie?" I ask, blinking hard.

I look at her in the rearview mirror and she shakes her head. "Pen," I say.

"No, Mom," she says, "I don't want to hear the rest."

"I know. I'm not going to say it. I just want you to know that I love you. Exactly as you are. I love how kind you are. I love how your body is flexible. I love how much you love reading, just like me. I love so many things about you. And I always have."

She is quiet for a minute. She puts her index finger in her mouth and looks out the window.

"Okay," she says. "You can tell the rest of the story."

She keeps her head down as I say it. "The doctors told us you had Down syndrome. And we were scared that it would hurt you and us. But it didn't."

She looks up with a smile. "But it didn't. And you were happy."

failure

I am struck by how sharing our weakness and dif-
ficulties is more nourishing to others than sharing our
qualities and successes.

—JEAN VANIER, *COMMUNITY AND GROWTH*

Becoming a mother has been as much about failure as anything
else.

It started in my imagination. I created a portrait of a good
mother, a portrait largely derived from my own mom, who could
have won prizes for the ways she followed the advice of *Family
Circle* and *Good Housekeeping*. I am the oldest of four girls, and
Mom kept us healthy and happy and wholesomely entertained
throughout our childhoods.

Take Halloween. Mom still has a Halloween album with
photos from every year of my youth. In the background, the
house has been turned into an orange and black extravaganza.
Up front, all four girls are decked out in creative, inexpensive,
homemade costumes. One year, we cut the shape of the conti-
nental United States out of a large piece of cardboard, painted
it according to the colors of the map on my wall, strapped it to
my chest, and then affixed Alaska to my head and Hawaii to my

index finger. Another year we dressed up as the weather. I was a cloud, Kate a rainbow, Brooks and Elly the sun and the rain.

Handmade pilgrims came out at Thanksgiving. The hallways overflowed with hearts in February. We drank green milk on St. Patrick's Day. Every Fourth of July involved a cake with Cool Whip, blueberries, and strawberries in the pattern of an American flag. And don't get me started on our house at Christmas.

It never dawned on me that all this creativity took a tremendous amount of time and effort. It just seemed like what good mothers were supposed to do.

Mom also offered an ideal of domesticity when it came to the day-to-day effort of managing a household. She cooked dinner for us every night. Yes, it occasionally included Spam, and there was one unfortunate run-in with a jar of fermented applesauce, but dinner with my mother never involved take-out pizza. Moreover, I grew up with a vegetable garden. Four plots in our backyard with wooden dividers and well-mulched paths, filled with lettuce and beans and squash and zucchini and tomatoes. I remember pulling the strings off the yellow wax beans in preparation for dinner. I remember rinsing dirt from the lettuce leaves. And those memories —of the gardens and the holidays and the home-cooked meals— are filled with laughter and peace and belonging.

So when I became a mother, I assumed that the ability, and the desire, to cook, garden, decorate, and sew Halloween costumes came with the territory.

Until I failed at all of the above.

* * *

The garden comes first. This third pregnancy seems to have summoned some latent domestic instincts. I decide to re-create one, just one, of the four plots of my childhood vegetable garden. I want to give our kids the experience of dirt and growth and bugs and bunnies. I have dreams of our whole family feeling more connected to the source of our food, even if only on a symbolic level. I envision vegetable casseroles and planting even more produce next year.

And then reality sets in. The crabgrass. The abundance of squash—all at once, growing so quickly I can't keep up, no matter how many casseroles we eat. The need for water almost daily. The tomatoes that never ripen. The parsley. I don't even like parsley. Or green beans, for that matter. After we pick them, they sit in a pile in the refrigerator until they are so shriveled I have to throw them away.

Stooping to pull out the crabgrass grows more and more uncomfortable as my stomach expands. Within a few weeks, I have failed as a gardener. I allow the weeds to overrun the vegetables, and eventually we dig up the whole plot and put grass in its place.

Fall arrives, and I try to put the gardening debacle behind me. One night, Penny and William are asleep, and Peter and I are cleaning up the dinner dishes. The house is quiet, but my mind is busy with lists and phone calls and goals for the season ahead, which includes my least favorite holiday.

"I'm thinking about Halloween," I say.

"Yeah," Peter replies, "I thought we could go to the consignment store and find something cute."

"I'm kind of opposed to store-bought costumes," I say in a tone that suggests offense, as if my husband has just proposed selling our unborn child to the highest bidder.

Peter looks at me with his eyebrows slightly raised. "You are also somewhat opposed to anything crafty."

It doesn't take me long to concede his point. I appreciate women who collect fabric scraps and own a glue gun, but that's just not me.

I soon realize I've put myself in an impossible situation. I'm convinced that Halloween is a big excuse for unnecessary expenditures and marketing peer pressure, so I don't want to spend any money on it. But my kids have costume parties at school, and I don't want them to miss out on the fun. I'm not objecting based on religious principles or something noble like that. The perfect solution would be for me to cobble something together by hand, but I don't have the time, energy, or skill required. I'm holding on to an ideal of mothering I can't achieve.

Up until now, I have managed to avoid the Halloween hype. We skipped Penny's first Halloween, sent her to my mother's for the second, and then Mom outfitted both kids—as Curious George and the man with the yellow hat, created from old dress-up clothes and props stored in her attic—the following year.

Last year, I improvised with some old costumes my sister and I had worn as a kid—a bunny and a carrot, which my mother had sewn by hand. The bunny costume was too big for Penny, and the thirty-year-old zipper was broken beyond repair. I affixed a few safety pins and rolled up the sleeves, and Penny ran around after William in his orange sweat suit and green hat pretending to eat him, and they had a fine time. I managed to spend no money on the holiday and still outfit my kids somewhat appropriately. Ideals upheld. More or less.

But this year, with the baby on its way and the supply of decades-old handmade costumes depleted, I fold. I purchase a doctor's outfit for Penny from Target. We affix a tinfoil badge to William's yellow rain jacket and call him a fireman.

Then Halloween Day arrives, and so does William's party at preschool, with his class's rendition of "Five Little Pumpkins" and a bat dance and pumpkin cupcakes.

That afternoon, William and I head to Penny's school. We cheer as the high school band plays for us all. We wave at Penny as she parades around the parking lot. The kids then march inside, and William and I walk down the hill to go home. When we return an hour later to pick up Penny for the day, I notice an unusual shortage of other students waiting for their parents. I don't think much of it until my friend asks, "How was the party in Penny's classroom?"

The what?

Later I say, "Penny, did other mommies and daddies come to your classroom after the parade?"

"Yes. Why weren't you there, Mom?"

I spend most of the night trying to answer that question. I still don't know why I wasn't there. I don't know if I missed a memo or if it was poor communication from the school. But I do know that if I'd had access to the tools monks invented for self-flagellation, I would have used them.

In the morning, Penny says, "Mom, next time don't forget the party."

I nod. "I won't."

She smiles. "Good. I love you, Mom."

And as far as Penny is concerned, that's that. She is disappointed, but she also seems to find my absence slightly amusing. What I see as failure she sees as an inconsequential oversight.

* * *

I think back to when Penny wanted tennis lessons. She noticed her dad heading out with his racquet, and she wanted to learn how to play. So Peter took her to watch some kids taking a lesson. They all were taller. They had all played tennis before. The group included a six-year-old boy who seemed to relish aiming the ball in the direction of the instructor's head. At the end of their observations, Peter said, "I'm not signing her up. I'll just teach her one-on-one."

Penny insisted. "Tennis lessons!"

We took her lead. She donned new tennis whites, and we bought a little racquet at Walmart. Penny was ready. Peter and I were worried.

The other kids hit the ball back and forth over the net. They moved their feet to position their bodies appropriately. They scampered around the court. Penny stood in place and turned her head as the balls bounced past.

I'm pretty sure that even at age four and a half, if I had been in Penny's shoes I would have finished every lesson feeling more and more discouraged. I would have considered myself a failure.

But every day when Penny walked off the court, she beamed.

"I hit the ball, Mom!" Sure enough, she had hit the ball, approximately one out of every ten times it came toward her.

"I was a good listener!" True—the instructor commented that Penny paid attention better than her older and abler peers.

At the end of the week, she summed it all up: "I did a great job!"

And as the list of "failures" in my life adds up—the vegetable garden, the take-out dinners, the Halloween costumes, the overlooked school events—I can't help but wish I could bring a little bit of my daughter to my own competitive, achievement-oriented, perfectionistic self.

* * *

Not long after my failed gardening attempt, William says, "Mom, why don't we have a garden like Nana's?"

A voice inside my head answers him: *Because I will never be the mother your grandmother was to me. Because I don't have time to watch small children and weed and prepare wholesome food. Because I like the farm stand up the road. Because I'm pregnant and I just can't handle everything I have to do each day as it is.* But another voice counters that I don't need to be so hard on myself. So I say, "Because there are some things I love and other things that Nana loves. That's why it's so wonderful you have both of us in your life."

William considers my explanation. Then he says, "I'd like to go to Nana's and help her pull out her weeds."

The next spring, William and Mom will plant a little garden in our backyard, with parsley, basil, and some pansies Penny has brought home for Mother's Day. They will tend it together. And every time I look at it, I will be grateful that I failed as a gardener.

heaven

Yes, people do find it hard to keep on feeling as if you believed in the next life: but then it is just as hard to keep on feeling as if you believed you were going to be nothing after death. I know this because in the old days before I was a Christian I used to try.

—C. S. LEWIS, *LETTERS TO CHILDREN*

"When we going see Grand Penny?" Penny asks. Our family has just arrived in New Orleans, her grandmother's hometown.

Her question surprises me. We talk often about Peter's mom, Grand Penny, and I thought Penny knew that her grandmother had died before she was born.

"Oh, sweetie," I say, "Grand Penny used to live in New Orleans, but she isn't here anymore."

Up north the leaves have begun to change color, but here the air feels moist, as if summer could show up at any moment. The city still bears the scars of Hurricane Katrina—clapboard houses display the spray-painted, fluorescent orange X-es from their assessment after the storm; empty lots testify to the fires that ravaged some neighborhoods; and the live oaks look more gray than usual, as if a blanket of ash has settled on them and is being sloughed off in gradual stages.

Penny says, "Oh. Otay." But she looks pensive, and I wonder whether for all these years she had thought Grand Penny was alive, just far away. I wonder what she thought this word "dead" meant.

"Sweetie, Grand Penny got really sick and she died. We won't see her again until we meet her in heaven," I say.

She nods.

The next day, Peter and I take Penny and William to Audubon Park. I have walked the two-mile loop around its perimeter countless times, but today we head to a new area. It is a labyrinth, a pattern etched into an expansive stone circle, with a path from the outer edges into the center.

For years, I had been skeptical of labyrinths. They conjured up myths and magic to me, occult spiritual practices at worst and false promises of emotional wholeness at best. But I had walked a labyrinth at a retreat center four years earlier, when I was worried about whether we would be able to have more children, and God had used that time as a way to healing. I remember the soothing rhythm, walking in and out, following a circuitous but clearly marked path, winding my way into the center and then retracing those steps out to the edges of the circle again.

Peter and I both approach the labyrinth with expectation this time, but I can't re-create my previous experience. As I try to keep my attention focused on the pattern, Penny and William are decidedly uninterested in the labyrinth's route. Instead, they gallop and jump and roll around, and I take delight in their boisterous energy. I love watching them together — Penny in her red corduroys and creamy-white cardigan, William with his V-neck navy blue sweater and a face that mirrors his father's. They hold hands. They giggle. They play.

I cut short my attempt at meditative walking and lead them over to the bench we are here to see. The inscription comes from a poem by Mary Oliver: "Tell me, what is it you plan to do with your one wild and precious life?"

"Penny and William," I say, running my fingers along the raised letters on the placard, "this is a bench for your Grand Penny."

Peter has entered the contemplative space of the labyrinth more than I have, but at this point he walks over to our trio and takes Penny in his lap. "Pen, do you know why you have the same name as Grand Penny?"

She shakes her head, her big eyes locked on his.

"Well, we wanted to show that there's a connection between who you are and who she was. It's a way of saying how much we loved her and also how much we love you." He tilts his head back. "Your Grand Penny would have loved you so much." His voice catches.

Penny says, "Hug her?"

Peter says, "One day. One day you can hug her."

She puts her head against his chest.

I think back to those months before Grand Penny died, and an old ache returns. Just after her death, that ache had seemed permanent, like a hole had opened up between my rib cage and my spine. By now, the grief has faded and the ache has disappeared, and I only remember it occasionally. But sitting here on the park bench, with Penny's hand in mine and Peter's eyes brimming, that space opens up once again. Like a bone that had broken and healed, but throbs every so often when a storm is on its way.

I close my eyes just for a moment to envision her, with her

high cheekbones and angular face balanced by a broad smile and sparkling eyes. I miss her. I miss the woman I knew when she was healthy—this woman who enjoyed kickboxing, who loved ice cream and didn't like cilantro, who had hand-addressed our wedding invitations. I miss the woman I came to know in the midst of her battle against cancer, who laughed so hard in response to a get-well card after surgery that the staples holding her wound together were dislodged, who walked around the block in sneakers and a nightgown just to get outside, who held my hand as she slept, who said thank you even at the very end.

I miss the woman she would have become as a grandmother, the woman who would have clapped with glee to watch William feeding the "quack quacks" at the pond, who would have sat cross-legged and summoned Penny into her lap to read a book, who would have spoiled the kids with treats and gifts and made them laugh with stories of their dad as a child.

I take a picture of Penny and William on the bench. Penny poses for the camera, batting her eyelashes and smiling. William looks away, ready to wriggle to the ground. Next to their faces an inscription reads, *In loving memory. Penelope Eaves Becker.*

* * *

Our children know that their grandmother died, and they know that we hope to see her again. They have watched the tears roll down our cheeks when we share memories of Grand Penny or when unexpected grief enters our home—the death of a colleague's son from cancer, the news of a friend's mom's sudden heart failure, the phone call about a classmate whose car hit a tree and killed the whole family. Still, they have no sense of the grief that comes with death.

In our household, we teach our kids that because God raised Jesus from the dead, we can trust Jesus' promise that we will join him in heaven. But this simple, hopeful narrative makes me wonder whether I am setting my children up for the shock that death still stings. We proclaim Jesus' triumph over the violence of the cross through the glory of the resurrection, but I wonder whether our kids will look back on our talk of heaven and think of it as pie in the sky, akin to Santa Claus and fairy tales. I wonder if I am betraying them with my words of healing and happiness and reunion to come.

My memory of Grand Penny's death involves beauty — as she reconciled with family members and worked to offer and receive forgiveness, as her body quieted when I sang "Amazing Grace," as she opened her eyes only for a moment after two days in a coma to say good-bye to her sons. But I also remember the brown fluid that flowed from her mouth and nose. The lumps under her skin. The urine and vomit. The horror of it.

The stories pile up if I look for them, stories of death by drowning, fire, cars, chemicals, storms. Stories of senseless, commonplace deaths of children, infants. When a baby dies, is there really a way to hold on to the promise of eternal life? When a child becomes an orphan, can Christians still proclaim the goodness of God? How can we cling to hope in the times when we see no signs of redemption?

I know the shadow of death. I have felt it, even if not as sharply as some. But if I have exposed my children to that shadow, it is only as a distant image, not a present reality. If death comes to visit them in the future — *when* death comes to visit them in the future — will they curse me for sheltering them from its brutality?

* * *

A few days later, Peter and I return from a walk in the park while the kids stay home with one of Peter's cousins. Penny asks, "Did you see Grand Penny?"

"No, sweetie," I say. "You know what happened to Grand Penny."

She gives me a small smile, but it isn't her natural look. She seems embarrassed that she had forgotten. Then she says, "Oh, that's right. She's in heaven. I'm fine with that."

"Why?" I ask.

"Because now she's all better."

I nod. It's what I have taught her to believe. It is what I hope I believe too.

At home, Penny and William have been stumbling their way through a Sunday school song that spells out the words "I will L-I-V-E-E-T-E-R-N-A-L-L-Y." It runs together as the song speeds up, and they don't know what the letters mean. But it is the promise that, with "C-H-R-I-S-T in my H-E-A-R-T," I will live forever. Because he lives, and because he invites me into that life.

Our kids have picked up on that iconic picture of heaven above the clouds and Grand Penny's spirit floating upward like a balloon that we watch and watch and watch until it disappears from sight. But the location of heaven remains a mystery to me. Beyond the clouds lies a cold, dark, immeasurable void. I imagine heaven as a spiritual dimension that we only catch in glimpses and whispers, a place outside time and space. And yet I hold to the promise from the Bible that heaven will also one day come to this earth, that a spiritual reality will supersede or envelop our physical reality so that the whole earth shimmers, filled with glory.

Perhaps I am giving my children a hope to which they can return in the years to come. Perhaps I am constructing a web of testimonies to the truth that though death raises an ugly and powerful head over and over again, life still triumphs.

She's in heaven. I'm fine with that. Because she's all better.

Perhaps they are giving that hope to me.

christmas

> There is nothing so secular that it cannot be sacred, and that is one of the deepest messages of the Incarnation.
>
> —MADELEINE L'ENGLE, *WALKING ON WATER*

William wakes up from his nap and says, "Mom, I want to talk."

He is in his crib, surrounded by his "sleep stuff," which includes two pacifiers, a stuffed giraffe, and a blue and green patchwork blanket. His hair sticks up at odd angles, and his eyes are a bit puffy. But the expression on his face tells me he has an agenda.

I settle myself in the chair across the room, resting my hands on my rapidly expanding midsection, and say, "What do you want to talk about?"

"Santa."

I shouldn't be surprised, even though we haven't made it to Thanksgiving yet. Talking about Santa has become a ritual. Every afternoon I lumber upstairs to find my son contentedly awake after two hours of deep sleep. When I come in, he doesn't want to get out of his crib. Rather, he's ready to chat. Often his questions head toward Santa, presents, elves, reindeer, and the North Pole. Then he returns to Santa and presents.

Today, as usual, I try to reframe the narrative. "You know, William, at Christmas, it's Jesus' birthday. We give presents to celebrate because Jesus was born, and Jesus loves us."

"Oh." He sucks on his pacifier for a moment, as if I have just offered new information, and then asks, "Does Santa love me?"

I put my hand to my mouth to cover my smile, but he is pondering the answer and doesn't notice. As much as I enjoy indulging William's imagination, I am also starting to sympathize with the Reformation sects that refused to celebrate Christmas. Apparently, even in the sixteenth century, this holiday seemed disconnected enough from its spiritual underpinnings for some Christians to abandon it altogether. At times I am tempted to do the same. For years now, I've had an internal battle waging over the nature of Christmas, and bringing kids into the picture has only made it feel more complicated.

* * *

When I first got married, I asked my mother for my box of Christmas ornaments. Peter and I lived in a shotgun apartment with twelve-foot ceilings, and I insisted on an eleven-foot tree for our first Christmas together. We hung the lights and filled in less than half of the available branch space with memories of my childhood — school photos in Popsicle-stick frames, needlepointed angels from my godmother, brass sleighs, glass baubles. But then we left for ten days. We returned after New Year's, with a lot of decorations to put away and a floor full of dry pine needles.

The next year, I decided a tree wasn't worth the effort if we wouldn't enjoy it on Christmas morning anyway. In the years that followed, sometimes I bought a wreath. Sometimes I hung the angels over the fireplace. But for the most part, I avoided the decorating and the baking associated with the long run up to December 25. It all seemed like a waste—of time, money, calories—and it seemed only barely related to a celebration of Jesus' birth.

But every Christmas, even as a married adult, I also gladly walked through the door of my childhood home, where my mother had been busily baking and decorating for weeks. There were the carolers in the front hallway—a different one to represent each member of the family. The little painted wooden snow scene in the window. Red bows on every closet door. Mistletoe hanging from the ceiling. Christmas china on the open shelves in the kitchen. Kooky cake and ham rolls and spinach casserole for the annual neighborhood Christmas party. "Joy to the World" and the "Hallelujah Chorus" and "Good King Wenceslas" playing round the clock. It was a time for feasting and celebration, and even though I often wondered what peppermint ice cream and garlands had to do with a baby born in Bethlehem, I loved it.

I finally decided that Christmas should be divided into two categories—"American Christmas" and "Christian Christmas." American Christmas involved Santa Claus and presents and eggnog and tinsel. Christian Christmas began with the mournful expectation of Advent and led to our celebration of Jesus' life. It made me feel better to divorce the two even as I decided to celebrate both.

When our kids were born, I continued to divvy up Christmas into my self-created sacred and secular categories. I tried to emphasize the sacred. The stuffed Nativity scene placed in the center of our playroom provided hours of entertainment. I wouldn't allow the kids to toss the baby, but the sheep and the donkeys were fair game. Someone sent us a sticker Advent series in which we read a portion of the Christmas story each day and placed a corresponding sticker on a scene that culminated, of course, in the babe lying in a manger. We sang "Christmas church songs" before bed, and one afternoon I overheard Penny singing, "God and sinners reconciled!" as we walked to the playground. Christian Christmas was sinking in.

It wasn't as easy for me to muster the energy or organizational effort for American Christmas. No carolers or festive china or place mats decorated with wreaths and snowmen. No glitzy bows. No "White Christmas" playing in the background. I put off shopping for so long that I often found myself up late, clicking on items online, paying extra for two-day shipping.

But festive place mats or not, there was Santa, who provoked fear and trembling in Penny and adoration in William. Penny asked about Santa all year round—whether to make sure he would stay put at the North Pole or in hopes that he might make a surprise early visit, I'm not sure. William homed in on all the details—Mrs. Claus, the size of the sleigh, the location of the factory. I started to worry that my kids loved Santa more than Jesus, that, despite all my efforts, American Christmas had gotten the best of us too.

* * *

Then comes this year, when I am pregnant for the third time and William can't stop asking about Santa's undying love for him. In December, Penny comes home from school one day singing and dancing to "Jingle Bell Rock." They have a performance coming up, and she practices daily. She knows every motion, and she sings loud and clear, if somewhat off-key. Her face is aglow with the light of a child who couldn't be more content or more excited.

It is at that moment that I start to wonder whether American

Christmas and Christian Christmas are more closely related than I had suspected.

I think back to the way Jesus' birth upended traditional assumptions that the spiritual world and the physical world must remain distinct spheres. Jesus' birth signaled the entrance of God into time and space. And despite Jesus' condemnation of evil, his life attests to his ongoing affirmation of the goodness of our physical reality. This is the man who changed water into wine so the party could continue. This is the man who commended a woman for pouring expensive perfume on his feet. The man who held the children on his lap rather than keeping them at a distance. The man who healed through touch and not just powerful words.

Christmas celebrates material reality, through gifts and glitter and extravagance. When we place the Nutcracker characters on the branches of our tree, when we bake molasses spice cookies, when we dress up in fancy clothes, we are acknowledging a spiritual truth made manifest on Christmas morn. We are participating in God's declaration that this world matters enough to enter into it, to upend the evil within it, to hold tight to the good, forever.

So first I concede that it wouldn't be a bad thing to start collecting Christmas ornaments. Embracing gift giving seems the next logical step, but I'm weary of our stuff. I don't want my kids to feel entitled to the new bike or book or toy. I don't want to fill another bin with items to give away. I think perhaps we should all pull names out of a hat and only give one gift apiece, or give the money to charity, or forget about presents altogether and just enjoy Christmas Day as a family.

Even as I entertain these possibilities, I keep circling back to the thought that gift giving is good. I know—buying my sister a sweater is a poor reflection of the gift God gave us in sending Jesus, but at least it's a tangible reminder of generosity.

And Christmas is also about receiving gifts. Instead of purchasing what I want for myself, I submit to what someone else wants me to have. At least in theory, receiving gifts prompts a recognition of all the things in life that come, not because of hard work or because we deserve it, but simply because we are loved. My children, who have no income, who depend on us for each bite of food and each piece of clothing and toy and book and game, know how to receive gifts. With simple joy. With great delight. With gratitude. The same way I want to receive God's gifts to me.

Which brings me to the final way my attitude has changed when it comes to Christmas. Perhaps because the theology of "Hark! The Herald Angels Sing" contrasts so starkly with the vacuous lyrics of "Holly Jolly Christmas," it was "secular" Christmas music that got me most of all.

Until Penny comes home singing "Jingle Bell Rock" with all her heart. And I realize there is no dividing line for her. Shaking those sleigh bells and belting out those lyrics are part of the celebration. After all, without Jesus' birth, there would be no reason to throw a party. It strikes me again that the whole point of Christmas, theologically speaking, is that the abstract became physical, the conceptual became concrete. For my children, for myself, it's important to celebrate Christmas, not only through words and hymns and spiritual practices, but through the embodiment of celebration and delight, through cookie swaps and presents around the tree and wreaths on the door. And, yes, through "Jingle Bell Rock."

* * *

A few days after Penny's holiday concert at school, we attend the early evening service at church. Peter roams the hallways with the kids, who have managed to sit still through two carols but not the Scripture reading. In the dim light of the sanctuary, I hear the story again, the story of a young girl entrusted with the Son of God, the story of shepherds awoken by glory, the story of the humble beginnings of a baby boy who would change the world and change my life. I rest my hands on my belly, that orb containing the life soon to be given to us. My family returns for "Silent Night," each person holding a candle, the whole room flickering with gentle light.

When we get home, Penny helps me read a child's version of the Christmas story out loud. As we narrate, William places each of the Nativity scene characters throughout the room for the rest of the relatives to see. First he perches an angel on the back of a wing chair. Then Mary, Joseph, and the donkey in the center of the coffee table. Then the animals and the shepherds on the floor around the table, the manger with the baby Jesus on the table itself. At the very end, as Penny and I read about the wise men, William lays two large American Girl dolls at the foot of the manger.

We all giggle, but then William, serious as can be, explains, "They are the presents from the wise men for baby Jesus."

He and Penny then lead us in a rollicking rendition of "Happy Birthday," and we bring out a cake. We all eat our fill.

We set out the cookies and milk for Santa. We leave the manger scene in its place.

We celebrate Christmas.

rest

The Sabbath, I said, is not only an idea. It is also something you *keep*. With other people. You can't just extract lessons from it.

—JUDITH SHULEVITZ, *THE SABBATH WORLD*

It seems like a good plan. A new year has begun, and the new baby will arrive soon, so we figure it is time for William to transition into a big-boy bed in the same room as Penny. We pave the way for the move with "sleepovers" once a week. On those nights William lies in bed across the room from his sister, straight as a board, and goes to sleep.

But when he starts having sleepovers night after night after night, William doesn't exhibit quite the same self-control. One evening, he pesters Penny so much that she eventually ends up in his crib upstairs just to get some rest.

A few minutes later, William approaches Peter and me in the kitchen. "I went upstairs to give Penny her water," he says. "She was sleeping. So I tiptoed."

"Great job, William," I say.

Peter nods and adds, "Now let's go to sleep."

William walks away but soon comes back downstairs.

"Before I gave Penny her water I 'pilled [spilled] it on my bed. Now everything is wet."

Fair enough. We drape his comforter over the stair railing and put the comforter cover in the dryer. William returns to bed. I stay with him until he falls asleep, reminding myself that all transitions take time.

Fast-forward three hours to midnight. I wake up and hear talking. I poke Peter, who finds William sitting up in bed, overhead light on, fan on, reading.

"I'm just having a little quiet time," he explains. "And I made the butterflies move." He points to the mobile overhead, spinning in circles from the fan's work.

Half an hour later, I take over for Peter. I hold William on my lap, rocking back and forth. I say, "William, what do you need to be able to sleep?"

"Mom," he says, "I need a fence."

The next night, we erect two child gates outside their door. Penny has proven adept at escaping with only one gate, so we figure another will help our cause. We plan to take the gates down once they are both asleep so the kids can reach us in the night if need be. Peter reads a story. I sing songs. We pray. We turn out the lights. William looks dazed and content under his baby blanket, cuddling his stuffed giraffe. Penny can hardly keep her eyes open. I hoist myself over the gates and stand around the corner to confirm that they have stayed in their beds.

Within sixty seconds, I hear Penny instructing William in her best imitation of a drill sergeant: "WILLIAM BECKER! You push that part right now! Push! Push! Push it down!" One gate topples. Penny's tone shifts. "Great job, William. I knew you could do it. Let's take a break and then we'll get the other one."

They escape in short order. From there come the requests. He needs to use the bathroom, legitimately. Next, "I need pajama pants." And a third time, "I need socks." Then there is a long lull, so I head downstairs to do the dishes. An hour later, I poke my head in to check on them. William is lying in bed, eyes open. He has raised the window blind, "for to look outside." He is a portrait of contentment, dressed in his Superman pajamas and, now, two of his sister's tutus.

At that, Peter puts him back in his crib. He needs a fence.

* * *

William's new bout of sleeplessness reminds me of the days when he was a very fussy infant who slept for intense spurts but never long stretches. Back then, I realized it took a fair amount of work for me to sleep as well. For years, I have gone to bed with some sort of white noise in the background, carried Tylenol PM with me when I travel, and preferred three pillows — one under my head, one between my legs, one behind my back. Beyond the physical props, most nights I can't fall asleep until I have made a list of all the tasks I should accomplish the following day. I keep index cards and a pen in my bedside table so I can jot down everything from "write blog post" to "order underwear for kids." I usually chart it out on a tentative schedule, just to give my brain some peace. Sometimes I need to map out the entire week.

I exhibit a similar sense of restless energy during the day, reading or writing emails or doing laundry or sorting clothes or preparing for my turn at the library's story hour or calling about the toilet seat that broke last week. I keep up with news by reading magazines while I'm blow-drying my hair or brushing my teeth or standing in line at the coffee shop. Even after the kids go to bed, I'm on the phone while packing their lunches or wiping down the counters in the kitchen while asking Peter about his day. When the time comes to actually rest, I don't know what that means. I don't know how to do it. And given the stories of other men and women I know — whether working in an office, at home with the kids, or some combination of the two — I'm pretty sure I'm not alone in my restlessness or in my weariness.

Perhaps, like my son, I need a fence.

* * *

A few years before William was born, I wrote a seminary paper comparing the two places in the Old Testament where God gives the Ten Commandments. For the most part, the two lists are the same. But not command number four, the one about keeping the Sabbath.

In Exodus 20, God commands rest in recognition of the work of creation: "For in six days the LORD made the heavens and the earth, the sea, and all that is in them, but he rested on the seventh day. Therefore the LORD blessed the Sabbath day and made it holy." Observing the Sabbath, here, is an act of worship. It is an invitation to remember God as Creator. To turn our attention fully to the one who made us, and to his pattern of being.

But in Deuteronomy 5, the commandment emphasizes that on the Sabbath day no one is to do any work. Not the Israelites, not their animals, not the people who work for them, not even the foreigners who live nearby. The reason given for this community-wide respite is that they — the workers and the foreigners, the "others" — should be able to rest "as you do." Here, the Sabbath is an invitation to the outsiders and the servants to participate in the blessings of life with God.

This version of the command concludes, "Remember that you were slaves in Egypt and that the LORD your God brought you out of there with a mighty hand and an outstretched arm." Here, as in the Exodus account, the Sabbath is an act of remembrance, but now it is an act of remembrance that extends outward. It is an invitation to care for other people.

I always appreciated the sentiment behind these commands, but it wasn't until I had children, and rest became harder and harder to come by, that I wanted to take this idea of a Sabbath day seriously. It seemed to be the only thing that might get me to slow down. But it also felt nearly impossible. There was just so much to do. Resting, even in response to God's gracious provision, seemed indulgent.

But then one Sunday we went to the grocery store after church because we were out of milk. And bacon. And bananas. And a whole long list of other items. Peter put Penny in one cart, and I put William in another. We divided and conquered and came home an hour later, trunk full. It felt great to get it all done—until I started to feel bad, not only because we had accomplished so much on Sunday, but also because I remembered back to that seminary paper and the command to rest on behalf of other people. I had implicitly asked a host of women and men to work in order to serve me.

I knew it was impractical to think that our whole culture would suddenly go back to the days of stores being closed on Sundays, and I knew that few, if any, individual workers would notice if I stopped shopping on Sundays. Resting on Sunday isn't what average Americans do, and part of me said that the biblical concept of Sabbath is a set of outdated commands, written for a people with different expectations for time and work and economic stability.

Still, I figured it would make some small difference, at least in my own life, to take one day to rest from asking other people to respond to my emails. To rest from being entertained. To rest from the grocery store and Target. And to understand that this rest is not just about satisfying my own need to slow down, but also about caring for the people around me.

At first, I just stopped shopping on Sundays. Those days served as a weekly reminder that everyone—the cashiers and bankers and doctors and janitors and teachers and bus drivers— was a person created in the image of God. It had been easy to behave as if the woman at the dry cleaning shop existed so that my clothes would be clean when I wanted them. It had been easy to reduce the life of the man restocking the grocery store shelves to his productive value. But refraining from shopping came as a reminder of the common grace that proclaims our value because of who we are as God's children and not because of what we have produced. When I started to take a day in which I didn't ask anyone else to work for me, the purpose of the Sabbath wasn't apparent only on Sundays. I also started to glimpse the image of God in the person in front of me when I stood in a checkout line on Monday morning.

Over time, the idea of a day of rest slid from a commandment to an invitation. I read about people who let their dishes and clothes stay dirty on Sundays to give the earth a partial rest from our use of electricity and water, and to give themselves a rest from all those chores. I read about others who prepared all their food on Saturday and then invited people over for a Sunday feast to celebrate together. I didn't put all these ideas into practice, but somehow, by taking seriously God's command to rest on behalf of other people, I began to learn how to rest as an act of trust and worship and thanksgiving.

I now look forward to Sundays—to a lazy morning as a family before the rush to get ourselves to church. I look forward to sitting in the pews together and taking a few moments to praise God, to pray with our community, to listen to a sermon and reflect on the truth it contains. Perhaps more than anything else I look forward to the afternoons, when most of our household falls asleep. Usually I spend time reading and journaling by myself. But almost always I end up with Penny or William cuddled beside me. They point out the sunlight through the trees in the backyard. They ask me how I met their dad. We read books. We rest.

* * *

Years ago, I spent a summer babysitting a three-year-old and a seven-year-old. One afternoon, I took them to the pool. I don't remember what happened to make the three-year-old, a little girl with long, curly blonde hair, erupt in tears. I just know that once she started wailing, I picked her up. She increased the volume of her screams and began to kick me. She thought I was trying to constrain her, when I only wanted to comfort her. I knew she couldn't calm herself, and yet holding her seemed only to make things worse. As her cries became shrieks, I started to sing. Softly, in her ear. Gradually, she settled down. The arms that had been a prison to her became what they were meant to be—an embrace. She laid her head on my chest and cried until she finally felt better. And then I let her go.

I thought of that incident recently when I read Psalm 23

and my eyes fell on the words that begin the second verse: "He makes me lie down." I remembered that little girl crying by the side of the pool. I remembered scooping her into my arms. Her resistance. My insistence. And eventually, her willingness to receive my care for her.

He makes me lie down.

He makes me.

But Psalm 23 doesn't end with God making the psalmist lie down. The action moves from *he makes me* to *he leads me* to *he restores me* to *he guides me*. It starts with God forcing the psalmist to take a rest, and it implies that the psalmist cannot "lie down" without God's intervention. Once he has rested, though, he can move forward in the presence of the God who is a guide, a healer, a protector.

God is teaching me how to rest, but it is still a struggle. Like that little girl I held so many years ago, I resist the embrace at the same time that I long for it. I hold on to my plans, my insistence that there isn't enough time, instead of turning with gratitude to the one who promises to hold on to me.

* * *

I finally let go of needing William to lie still and quiet in his big-boy bed. Instead he stays in his crib throughout my pregnancy. We will put the new baby in a bassinet until her big brother is ready to relinquish his spot. He will learn how to rest. And we will continue to make him lie down.

disability

A *syndrome* means, at root, a "running together."
When you have a child, it all runs together: the heart
defect, the eyes, the way her voice sounds, the name
of the speech therapist, the worries over the future,
the joys of discovery, the sliding sense — slow, quiet,
enormous, an avalanche in the skull — that different is
not as different as you thought.

—GEORGE ESTREICH, *THE SHAPE OF THE EYE*

I am sitting in the living room with William. We finish reading
Library Lion, and he leans his head against my shoulder.

"Mom," he asks, "what *down syn* mean?"

I squeeze his leg and give it a pat, a signal that I am ready to
get up. I say, "*Down syndrome*, sweetie. Not *down syn*."

"I know *drum*," he replies. "What *down syn* mean?"

I nod slowly and sit back in my seat, realizing he has envisioned making music every time we have mentioned his older
sister's diagnosis. So I say, "Well, syndrome is all one word, and
it doesn't have anything to do with an instrument." I think back
to earlier in the day, as we were driving Penny to preschool and
I told her there would be another little boy with Down syndrome

joining her class. I try to picture what William has in his head—
two children carrying the same types of drum?

What down syn mean?

I scroll through the past five years of my own learning process, searching for words to explain a chromosomal anomaly to
a two-year-old. I decide to start with the biology. I say, "It means
Penny has an extra part in her body," but then I realize it sounds
as though she might grow a third arm. So I pivot and try, "It's
something that makes Penny special."

He sticks out his lower lip. "I want to be special."

I hug him tight. "You are, sweetie. You and Penny are both
very special."

He doesn't ask any more about it, but I puzzle through what
I could have said differently. I could have tried to explain the
words themselves—that Down syndrome is the layman's term
for trisomy 21, a third copy of chromosome 21, usually in every
cell of a person's body. I could have shown him Penny's karyo-
type, the graphic representation of her chromosomal makeup,
which includes three stubby lines clustered together like a trio
of old men squatting side by side. I could have told him that it is
probably because of Down syndrome that Penny wears glasses
or probably because of Down syndrome that she is short. Even
those details become complicated, though, when I think of her
as the third generation of women in my family with glasses at a
young age, or when I recall that I was always the smallest person
in my class at school. And I wonder whether any of that information would tell William anything more about who his sister
is or what her life means than what he already knows—that
she is his "super-great friend" who is learning how to read and
pump herself on the swing, who holds his hand when he is afraid

of loud noises, who wrestles with him and fights with him and loves him.

I think about how other people might answer the same question. If William decided to ask around, he might hear that Down syndrome means Penny is an angel sent from God to teach us something. He might hear that she is a genetic mistake who drains our country's educational and health care resources. But glorifying her or vilifying her doesn't match up with our experience either. There are days when she is the loveliest child I've ever met—when she runs to my side and says, "Hug!", when she asks, "How was your day, Mom?", when she wants to pray for someone who is sick. But she is no more sweet or loving than William. She tests my limits and disobeys and deceives me about her intentions in equal measure.

Although he might not be able to put it into words, I suspect if anyone tried to tell William that Penny is more or less significant than he is, he would know those grown-ups didn't get it right. It's not just that their perceptions don't match the reality of who Penny is. William already understands what it's taken me a long time to believe—that generalizations and assumptions rarely match reality for any of us.

* * *

When William was six months old, a family came to visit. This family included a teenager with Down syndrome. Sarah wasn't able to speak very many words. She used a few signs to communicate her needs and wants. She carried a doll around with her wherever she went. She was very polite. As I interacted with her throughout the evening, I kept coming up with all the things she couldn't do. She couldn't read. She couldn't drive a car. She couldn't have a conversation.

After dinner, we moved into the playroom, and I set William on his back on the floor. William was tough at that point in his life. He cried a lot. He squirmed a lot. He never cuddled, and his body was rarely, if ever, calm. As soon as I placed him on the floor, he started to kick and punch the air. But then Sarah sat down with him, and it was as if the embodiment of peace had come to visit. He lay there for a good fifteen minutes as she gently stroked his cheek and smiled. I had never seen him so content.

I talked with Sarah's mother later about that interaction, and she said, matter-of-factly, "Oh, yes, that's Sarah's gift." She went on to tell me of the time when Sarah was two years old and had gone over to a member of their church and had climbed into her lap. Sarah's mom came in to find the woman with tears streaming down her cheeks because Sarah, using no words, was comforting her. She told another story of a woman in a nursing home who was prone to harsh language and slapping people away when they tried to touch her. When Sarah and her mom were at the nursing home to visit someone else, Sarah went right up to this abusive woman and put her hand on her. The woman slapped her hand away. Sarah put it back. She slapped it away. Sarah did it again and again and again until the woman was willing to receive her touch. Sarah covered this woman's hand with kisses until her body became calm and she silently wept.

Sarah-in-general fits what a textbook would tell me about disability. Sarah-in-particular is a whole different story. When I try to explain to William what Down syndrome means, what disability means, I want to do so only in the context of knowing people's stories.

* * *

Not long after our discussion of "down syn," William comes home from school and says, "Mom." He says it as a sentence, the way he does when he has something important to tell me. And then again. "Mom. My friend Ashley is not good at listening. And she screams."

William attends a local public preschool as a student in the same "integrated" classroom that Penny attended two years earlier, where students with some form of disability learn side by side with their typically developing peers.

We were delighted when William was accepted, via lottery, into that class. But I wondered if I would be able to put words to his experience. I wondered if I would be able to help him see Ashley (and Carlos and Megan and Landon) as his peers. I wondered if I would be able to talk about disability in a way that was honest and positive, in a way that built bridges instead of creating categories or judgments. So when William tells me that Ashley doesn't listen well and screams, I take a deep breath.

I say, "Maybe she hasn't learned how to listen yet."

He nods.

I ask, "What is Ashley good at?"

He tilts his head. "Playin' games and runnin' around."

"What are you good at?"

"Listening."

"What's hard for you?"

"Coloring."

William doesn't notice what has happened in our conversation—that we have been able to draw parallel lines between him and his friend rather than emphasizing their differences or her special needs. As the year goes on, William talks about Ashley, but only because he tells me things about his friend—that she takes the bus, that they pretend to do cooking together, that he wants to have a sticker chart with prizes, just like she does. As far as William is concerned, Ashley is just another kid in his class. Some things are challenging for her. Some things she's good at. Just like him.

* * *

I work hard to put disability in positive or neutral terms for my kids. If we see someone using a wheelchair, we talk about how the wheelchair helps that person get around, just like our legs help us. When Penny goes to school with a little boy who hasn't learned to speak, we talk about the other ways he communicates—with his hands and his eyes and his iPad. We also talk about some of the benefits of that extra chromosome Penny has. As William could tell you, Penny is much more flexible than he is. She can put her nose to her shins with her legs straight out. She also seems to have lost the competitive gene that got passed on to every other member of our family. And whether this character trait comes from Down syndrome or something else, Penny's generous spirit is a gift to us all.

Still, Penny struggles to do math problems and she can't keep up with other kids in a game of tag and it hasn't been easy for her to make friends. Potty training lasted for years. I know the route to the nearest children's hospital by heart. And there are times when I hear other people talking about their kids' futures—college and marriage and grandchildren—and, with a wave of sadness that reminds me of the early days of her life, I realize how unknown the future is for her. Sometimes I worry that what our culture says is true, that people with disabilities are worse off than the rest of us. Sometimes I wonder if I should do more to teach my kids the harsh reality of a society in which many believe that productivity defines us and IQ correlates to personal worth.

But then I think about Jesus. The gospels don't record any interactions between Jesus and someone with an intellectual disability that we know of, but they give us many examples of how Jesus treated people on the margins—women, blind and deaf men, children, beggars, lepers. In each case, Jesus treats them as individuals. He refuses to join the disciples in categorizing a blind man as a sinner. He refuses to heal the bleeding woman without speaking to her face-to-face. He not only heals people but also works to restore them to their particular religious or social communities.

Perhaps what is most remarkable about Jesus' posture toward individuals who we might call "disabled" is that it is the same as his posture toward everyone else. He makes no distinction for people with disabilities. He sees brokenness. He sees need. He sees possibilities. He sees belovedness. He treats every one of them, every one of us, with the dignity every child of God deserves.

* * *

I am still considering William's question about "down syn" when I meet a young woman with a younger brother who has Down syndrome. I sit in a coffee shop with her, the baby wriggling and kicking inside me, and I tell her my story, the many months it took for me to receive Penny as a gift. I ask her about growing up with a sibling with a disability. She says, "I never knew the world any other way. For you, there's a before and after. For me, this has just always been our family. I've always loved my little brother. It's really normal." She shrugs, almost apologetic at the simplicity of her answer. "That's kind of all there is to it."

Later that day, Penny and William and I bundle up for a walk outside. As we head down the road, I say, "Hey guys, I had coffee today with a girl who has a brother with Down syndrome just like Penny."

William has never returned to the specific question of what Down syndrome means, and I'm not sure I would try to give him an answer if he did. I'm not sure I have an answer myself. But on this day, Penny pumps her fist in the air and says, "I've got Down syndrome!"

William tries to imitate her, pumping his own fist in the air and saying, "I don't have Down syndrome!"

They erupt in laughter and start to run ahead of me, hand in hand.

Jesus

The Lord did not come to make a display. He came to heal and to teach suffering men. For one who wanted to make a display the thing would have been just to appear and dazzle the beholders. But for Him Who came to heal and to teach the way was not merely to dwell here, but to put Himself at the disposal of those who needed Him.

—ATHANASIUS OF ALEXANDRIA, *ON THE INCARNATION*

Today held the winter's first snowstorm. As I help William get ready for bed, I glance out his third-floor window, and, despite the inky darkness, light bounces off the white ground and blankets the trees. I am far too pregnant to play in the snow, but today we stood on the back porch and stuck our tongues out to catch snowflakes, and we built a fire and drank hot chocolate and played with trucks and read stories. I am thinking about the simple goodness of all these things when William asks, "Mom, why this diaper different?"

It takes me a minute to realize that this new box of diapers has a different color fringe, blue instead of purple. I shake my head, amazed by his attention to detail and say, "William, where did you come from?"

He is lying on his back, looking up at me. "From God." He says it matter-of-factly, as if he is surprised I don't know.

"Who told you that?" I ask, pretty sure this answer hasn't come from me.

"Jesus," he says, in the same tone.

"Really?"

"Yes. Sometimes at night Jesus sneaks into our house. And I listen."

I don't know what to say.

* * *

When I was fifteen years old, I had an encounter with God that changed my life. But it took nearly a decade for me to feel comfortable talking about Jesus.

I had grown up attending church, so I could have recited plentiful Bible stories and even some theological points about Jesus' birth and death and resurrection. I had been baptized as an infant and confirmed my membership in the church while I was in middle school. I went to youth group and lived by Christian moral standards, as much as I could understand them.

But it wasn't until I was fifteen that I felt a longing for God. In the spring of that year, I was diagnosed with a rare condition called gastroparesis. In layman's terms, my stomach was paralyzed. I was so sick that I spent a week in the hospital. I completed the spring term from home. I spent the better part of four months on our couch in the family den, reading Dickens and Hardy to keep up with English class, puzzling through our physics textbook, and wondering whether I should go back to boarding school at all.

Everything felt uncertain. My friends were far away. I had

applied for leadership positions at school that I probably wouldn't get anymore. The school administrators were talking about having me repeat my sophomore year, so my grades seemed irrelevant. Worst of all, I had left school ten days before I was supposed to perform as the lead in the school play. For the first time, if this God I had heard about in church was real, then I was interested in finding out what he was up to. And so I started to pray, as if God existed, and as if God might care about my life.

Throughout that spring, kids who I had met the summer before through our church youth group came to visit me. The days outside had turned warm. The daffodils were blooming. These new friends could have been throwing a Frisbee at the beach, but instead they were visiting me—the outsider, the sick one. During those months if I stood up too quickly, I passed out. My brain felt sluggish, and it took effort even to smile. But these kids acted as if they enjoyed my company. I couldn't understand it.

As the weeks went on, I became more and more uncertain about going back to school. I thought it might make more sense to stay home, with these new friends and a church youth group close at hand. So I decided to ask God what to do, and when I asked, I heard a specific answer: "Go back to boarding school, and take me with you."

After that moment, I prayed regularly. I blazed through the New Testament. I read books that offered "evidence" of miracles and defended the accuracy of the Bible and testified to the historicity of the resurrection. I attended every Bible study I could find. And I returned to boarding school, ready to tell anyone who would listen that God cared about us.

But Jesus remained an enigma. Both God the Father and the

Holy Spirit seemed appropriately grand, abstract, and mysterious. I liked the vastness of a universal creator. But a God who came to earth in the form of a baby boy? I believed it, I guess, but I didn't know what to think about it. I certainly didn't want to talk to other people about it. I would happily debate the existence of God, the reality of answered prayer, the concept of a Spirit who inspired the Bible and wanted to guide our everyday life. But talking about a "personal relationship with Jesus" twisted my gut.

In retrospect, I think I worried about the exclusiveness of it all. If God had actually entered time and space as a baby, then the Christian religion, and truth and hope and joy and grace, all hinged on this one Jewish baby boy. Other religions had insights that seemed compatible with Christianity. Islam acknowledged similar standards of truth and goodness; Judaism included forgiveness and grace; and plenty of other faith traditions told stories of rapturous experiences of worship, not to mention the common causes of justice and compassion for those in need. But if what the Bible said about Jesus was true, then all those other religions were shadows of the reality contained in this one person. I believed in the particularity of Jesus, the "one and only-ness," but I didn't like the implications of my belief. It felt presumptuous to say that in knowing Jesus I knew the only way, or even the best way, the fullest way, to experience the divine.

Still, somewhere along the line, I fell in love. It was as if God took me by the hand and gently led me, like a little child, to meet the one I had been avoiding. After years reading and rereading the Pentateuch, the Prophets, and Paul's letters, I returned to the gospel stories, and I encountered a man who preached and healed and loved people, all sorts of people. I wondered if he could love me like that too.

The stories of Jesus' tenderness piled up until I had a reservoir of kindness and truth and generosity to circle back to again and again—Jesus stopping not only to heal a woman who has been bleeding for twelve years but also to look into her eyes and call her, "Daughter" ... Jesus teaching the prominent religious rulers of his day and yet welcoming the interruption of a man who can't walk and is plunked down at his feet ... Jesus cooking breakfast for his disciples ... Preaching blessing on the sorrowful, the vulnerable ... Multiplying the loaves and fish, not as a miraculous display of power, but as compassionate provision for those in need ... Opening his arms to the children, even when his disciples assume they are a nuisance ... Inviting himself to dinner at the house of a man everyone else scorned ... Sitting down by a well with an outcast woman ...

As I read, I started to wonder whether the particularity of Jesus was an invitation more than an offense, an unfathomable welcome to all the daughters and sons of the earth into the household of God.

* * *

When Penny was two, we started reading stories about Jesus from a large picture book that narrated events from the gospels in simple language with colorful graphics. Every day for months, we flipped through the pages until she had memorized parts of the stories of Zacchaeus and Bartimaeus and the good Samaritan. But one day, she put her hand on top of the page, as if to stop me from reading further. "See Jesus, Mama. See Jesus."

I pointed him out in the picture. His back was to us.

She shook her head. "See Jesus. See Jesus."

We flipped through every Jesus story, only to discover that the illustrator never portrayed Jesus' face. Penny wasn't satisfied until I went online and produced a portrait of Jesus. She smiled. We could go back to reading the book now.

William never fixated on seeing Jesus, but he enjoyed stories about Jesus just as much as his sister. Once, when I was scheduled to read to his preschool class, I asked him to select a book. He raced into the playroom. When he returned, he said, "Mom, I picked the Jesus book. Because I don't think my friends have learned about Jesus yet."

It was such a simple statement. He didn't want his friends to convert to Christianity. He wasn't thinking about evangelism or sin and salvation. He just wanted to share some stories about this person named Jesus whom he was getting to know. But I worried that the book would put his teachers in an uncomfortable position. Truth be told, I worried it would put *me* in an uncomfortable position. I convinced him to select something else instead.

But there it was again, a child's perspective on Jesus as someone attractive. Someone to tell your friends about. Someone who talks to the ones who will listen.

* * *

I assume one day my kids will ask me the questions that used to plague me—whether their friends who aren't Christians will go to heaven, what happens when babies die before they can profess faith, what happens to people in other countries who have never heard of Jesus. I will do the best I can to respond, but my answer will mostly come not from theological arguments but through an invitation. I will point them back to Jesus, the one who is "the image of the invisible God," the one who hates injustice yet loves sinners, the one who welcomes the adulteress and the righteous leaders, the one who held little children and healed the sick, the one who told jokes and riddles and taught us to think about God as our Daddy. The one Matthew's gospel calls "God with us."

I will point them to the shepherds that first night in Bethlehem, common laborers on the outskirts of town, charged with bearing witness to the grandeur of God. I will point them to the disciples, a motley crew of tax collectors and fishermen who bickered with each other about power and status as often as they displayed devotion or piety. And to the women who came to the empty tomb, who held the responsibility of proclaiming the resurrection, even though back then their word would not count in a court of law. I will remind my children, and myself, that we are just as ordinary, and just as treasured, as they were.

I will also remind them that though we can try to relate what God has done in Jesus, like the shepherds, like the women at the tomb, we cannot convince others that it is true. We can only invite them to come and see.

* * *

Not long after William tells me that Jesus sneaks into his room at night, I am praying with Penny before I turn out her light. After I conclude the prayer, Penny asks, "What *in Jesus' name* mean, Mom?"

It has been a long day. We have friends over for dinner, and I want to get downstairs to a glass of wine and some adult company as quickly as possible. I've already fallen for three other stalling tactics (water, socks, and prayer), so I say, "Um, it's just the way we pray, Pen. Okay?" I give her a kiss and walk out the door.

But her question lingers. What does it mean to offer a prayer to God—to converse with God and believe that God hears and responds—in the name of Jesus?

A few days later, Penny and I are sitting on the living room sofa, looking out the picture window at Peter and William building a snowman. I say, "Pen, I didn't answer your question very well the other night."

"That's okay, Mom."

"I know, but I'm going to try to do better. You asked me what it means to pray in Jesus' name. And I've been thinking about your question. I think it means we aren't just praying on our own. We are praying as a part of Jesus' family, in Jesus' name." I open my arms to indicate her brother and her dad in front of us. "Just like our family all has the name Becker, God's family all has Jesus' name. So when we say, in Jesus' name, we're saying that we're excited to be a part of God's family."

As I say it, I realize that I have become more and more like my children. I want to tell my friends about Jesus in the same way I want to talk about the novel I just finished reading or the new restaurant we enjoyed, not out of obligation, but out of delight. There is so much I do not understand, and so many questions that have remained unanswered. But after all these years of trying to nail down the specifics, trying to hold on to the arguments that will convince others, convince myself, of Jesus' divinity, I am ready to simply be with him.

I am glad he sneaks into our house. I hope I have ears to listen.

beauty

In Jesus, we notice a body that is not an object in itself, but one that moves toward others in love. We see a body that is made, not to be viewed, but for relationship. Just like ours.

—MARGOT STARBUCK, *UNSQUEEZED*

I have never been a cute pregnant woman. As someone who barely breaks the five-foot mark as it is, there's not much room to fit thirty-plus pounds of additional fat and fluid and baby. The third time around, it only gets worse. I have looked large throughout this pregnancy, and people have felt free to tell me what they see: "You must be having twins!" "They must have the due date wrong." "You can't be only six months pregnant; you're too huge."

Now we are nearing the end, and with my due date in sight, Peter and I go out to dinner. Two full tables of people stop conversation and crane their necks to watch me waddle past. I hear a man whisper, "Don't say anything," as he stares.

I remember women in Southern novels who stayed in their houses for the final month of pregnancy because it would be inappropriate to show themselves in public. Maybe they had the right idea.

When I look up this stage in *Your Pregnancy Week by Week*, I find this: "It would be unusual for you not to be uncomfortable and feel huge at this time. Your uterus has filled your pelvis and most of your abdomen. It has pushed everything else out of the way. At this point in pregnancy, you may think you'll never want to be pregnant again because you're so uncomfortable."

The facts don't help me feel any better. I swallow back the admonitions that I should have done more to stay in shape, should have exerted some self-control when my body demanded more pizza, should have been able to remain petite and adorable instead of ballooning into the biggest version of me I have ever known. Lying in bed at night, I return to the comments about my size and come up with equally rude but witty comebacks. And yet the guilt, the shame, the anger — it all leaves me with a sense of heaviness on my shoulders, as if I am a marionette whose strings are suddenly pulling me toward the ground.

But in the midst of what feels like a constant barrage of criticism come my children. They marvel at my size, but somehow their comments feel different. They take comfort in my soft curves. Their words about my body are filled with wonder. They run their hands across my "big belly," pulling away when the baby kicks, then coming close to whisper a message.

Many days, William says, "You look pretty, Mom." And he gives me a hug.

And I find myself wanting to see what my children see. I want to learn how to see myself through the eyes of love.

* * *

Two years earlier, I was getting ready to go out to dinner with Peter. Penny sat on the floor nearby. I had shed my shorts and

T-shirt and had chosen a skirt from the closet. I reached for a sweater, but then I caught a glimpse of myself in the full-length mirror mounted to the back of the door. I stood there, half clothed, assessing the state of my body. I eyed the fat that had settled around my middle now that William had stopped nursing. I noted the shadows under my eyes, the lines that ran like train tracks across my forehead. I had barely entered my thirties, but all at once I had started to feel old.

Then Penny, sitting nearby, lifted her head from a book and said, "Booful, Mama," with a wide smile and soft eyes. And something fluttered inside my chest.

Is that what you see?

"Thank you, sweetheart," I said.

She returned to her book, but my gaze had shifted to my daughter. I began to think about that word, the word I had used to describe her over and over again in the years since she arrived, with her sparkling green eyes, her rosebud lips, her porcelain skin: *beautiful.*

* * *

After Penny was diagnosed with Down syndrome at birth, I didn't see her much for the next two days. There were tests to run, and they needed to keep her under warming lights for her jaundice. Even when she was in my arms, I was looking for the physical attributes that the doctors told us would be different in her than in most people I knew. The epicanthal fold, an additional layer of skin around her eyes. The small, flat features, and loose joints, and the tongue that seemed too big for her mouth. The horizontal line that ran from one side of her palm to the other.

It took a few months for me to realize how much the doctors hadn't told me about my daughter. They hadn't told me she would have black eyelashes that curled as though she had spent the afternoon getting her makeup done. Or that I would pull out photos of Peter as a baby and think she looked just like him. Or that, like many people with Down syndrome, her eyes would have Brushfield spots—flecks of sparkling light, drawing me in like jewels shimmering in sunlight. And the doctors hadn't told me how her hair would frame her round cheeks or that her hands, always so small, would be so soft, so lovely.

I could name the attributes that made Penny beautiful. I could defend her beauty against any list of physical features that might imply otherwise. But she wasn't beautiful because of her features. The other thing the doctors hadn't told me was that I would love her, and that we can always see the beauty in the ones we love.

I saw Penny's beauty from the moment she was born, and I saw it as she grew. I just hadn't realized that she saw the same thing when she looked at me.

* * *

When I had gastroparesis in high school, and my stomach was paralyzed, I saw my illness as great news. I could eat whatever I wanted and regurgitate my food and tell myself I didn't have an eating disorder. Healing, both physically and emotionally, took years.

Throughout my illness—even as I kept a record of every fat-free cookie, every apple, every cup of frozen yogurt I consumed—I longed for freedom from the pressure to stay thin. I taped Bible verses to my mirror, index cards that read, *Your body is a temple of the Holy Spirit* and *Man looks at the outward appearance, but the Lord looks at the heart* and *Your beauty should not come from outward adornment ... Rather, it should be that of your inner self, the unfading beauty of a gentle and quiet spirit ...* The verses didn't change my behavior or my attitude. But I wanted to believe them. I longed for the day when I wouldn't worry so much about the number on the bathroom scale or the way my jeans fit.

Back then, I thought growing up and having kids would usher me into a new era of loving my body. I actually looked forward to having a body and face marked by the passage of time. I looked to my grandmother as a model of what my body would one day become. Her body told stories, and they were stories we loved. I saw her sunspots as reminders of countless happy afternoons on the beach, her wrinkles as testimonies to laughter, to worry, to a husband who left her a widow at age twenty-eight. The stout waist proclaimed her children. The miscarriages. The three who lived.

When we were with her, we sang songs from old musicals and listened to her tales of beaus and parties and volunteering during the war and hiding her engagement to my grandfather from her parents. We climbed on her lap and snuggled in close. She seemed to enjoy our curiosity about her weekly manicures and visits to the hair salon and her ritualistic way of applying lipstick. But she also indulged us when we asked her to extend her arms, as if she were pretending to fly. She even laughed when we got what we wanted—the chance to jiggle the extra skin and fat under her triceps as if it were a guitar string we could pluck. I now understand she would have gladly shed some pounds and returned to the smooth skin of her youth, but to me she seemed blessedly at ease in her body. I always saw her as beautiful.

I admired women like my grandmother, so I expected to one day be proud of my laugh lines, to shrug my shoulders at the loose skin around my neck. I envisioned holding on to the extra layer of fat around my middle and calling it "love handles," with a smile. As a self-conscious teenager, I had thought I would receive my aging body as a badge of honor and a chance to stop caring about the gaze of the world. I thought that once I had given birth, I wouldn't mind when a bathing suit no longer looked good. I thought I would be able to see it as a worthwhile tradeoff: I don't have a flat stomach, but I do have a family. I do have a past.

But when it comes time to embrace my aging self, I still critique what I see far more than I celebrate it. My body has expanded and shrunk, and, like a rubber band used a few times, my skin hangs a little. I have extra pounds that refuse to budge, no matter how many crunches or yoga routines or Stairmaster workouts I do. My face hints at more lines to come, lines that will connect me to my parents — the same lines that create a parenthesis around my father's mouth, those that radiate from my mother's eyes.

I live in a culture of perpetual youth, and it feels almost rebellious to choose to grow plump and wrinkled and gray. I find myself both tempted and repelled by the options of age-defying cream and hair coloring and intense aerobic exercise well into my golden years. And I wonder whether increased hours at a spa and time at a gym will ultimately keep me from the kind of beauty I have always hoped for, an unselfconscious beauty, a beauty that begins not with lotions and perfumes and abdominal workouts, but with wholeness and peace and laughter. A beauty that begins with love.

* * *

After that moment with Penny, I tried to talk myself into accepting an older, softer version of me, but self-criticism still came more naturally. I set a goal of running in a ten-mile race. I didn't even make it to the four-mile version. I routinely snacked on potato chips instead of carrots. I chose sleep or snuggling with the kids or reading instead of a morning workout. And though I attempted to reason myself through those decisions with admonitions that I didn't need to hold on to my youth any longer, I still wanted to looked different. And now, in the late stages of my third pregnancy, I am appalled at my body even as I wish I could embrace it.

Throughout it all, my children gaze at me with delight. They love to watch me apply makeup, and they beg me to give their hair a blast from the hair dryer. We have created a dress-up bin piled high with costumes from princesses to superheroes, but my closet remains their favorite trove of clothing. I routinely discover Penny in my high heels. They steal my necklaces. They wear my sweaters. And they revel in the parts of my body that give me pause.

They see me as I saw my grandmother. They see me through the eyes of love.

Perhaps someday I will join them.

Booful, Mama.

prayer

God also cheers when we come to him with our wobbling, unsteady prayers. Jesus does not say, "Come to me, all you who have learned how to concentrate in prayer, whose minds no longer wander, and I will give you rest."

—PAUL MILLER, *A PRAYING LIFE*

William's body flows in and out of my peripheral vision as he rolls on the carpet, climbs the bottom bunk, and slides back down with a thump. Peter and I are sitting on the floor in the kids' room, trying to usher in some semblance of peace. This is night three of a renewed attempt to introduce regular bedtime prayers. This baby will arrive any day now, and I would prefer to be getting myself ready for bed. But I also like the idea of praying together, and I figure William will pay attention eventually.

Penny took to this idea immediately. For the third night in a row, she is lying still, knees tucked under her torso, face to the ground. I don't know where she came up with this posture, but what her body communicates is clear. She is ready to pray.

Peter and I offer some simple words, asking for God's presence and help, and then it is Penny's turn. I can only understand snippets, something along the lines of, *Thank you for our day and William got a fever today and school was fun and we ate chocolate cake. Chocolate cake! And thank you for our family and all the people and Nana and Pop Pop coming this weekend and a fair! Animals at a fair! And help us all love.* Her intonation helps me guess the content—lilting and happy, intensifying for a moment, and back to happy again. She talks to God for longer than she has ever talked to either of her parents in her five years of life. Then she looks up at us, with an expression that seems almost bashful. *Amen.*

For the next few weeks, whenever Peter and I ask her questions about her day, she shrugs her shoulders or gives one-word answers. We aren't sure if she can't remember what happened at school or if she just doesn't want to talk about it or feels pressure from us when we put her on the spot. But in prayer, she talks and talks and talks. Somehow it offers her a sense of safety that our dinner conversations can't provide.

I wonder how much she understands. So I ask, "Penny, when you pray, what are you doing?"

She looks at me with her forehead wrinkled, as if she can't figure out why I need to ask the question. "Talking to God, Mom."

* * *

I said prayers as a kid. I vaguely remember kneeling by the side of my bed with my mother, trying to recall the words of prayers she taught us. I don't think I ever prayed on my own. Prayer was something for church and part of my bedtime ritual.

Eventually, my faith became more real, more personal. By

the time I was in my twenties, my morning routine involved reading the Bible, writing in my journal, and praying. But once my children were born, it seemed that whenever I set my alarm to try to steal a few contemplative moments, the kids woke up earlier. My personal prayer time fell by the wayside.

I still wanted prayer to be a part of my children's lives, so I tried to offer them a little instruction. One night, with William asleep in his crib upstairs, I was putting Penny to bed, and I said, "I want to teach you a prayer."

She sat up and put her hands together.

I said, "I'll say a line, and then you repeat it."

"Otay."

"Our Father," I started, but then I opened my eyes and interrupted myself. "Penny, did you know that God is our father just like Dad is your father? Well, in a similar way ..."

I had a little debate in my head at this point, wondering, *Is it a fact that God is our father, or is it a metaphor? Should Penny grow up thinking of God as her father? As our father? As anyone's father?* This was more complicated than I'd thought.

I decided "Dear God" would do.

She repeated, "Dear God."

"Who art in heaven ..." I stopped myself again. "Well, God does live in heaven, but God is also here with us right now."

By the time I tried to explain "hallowed," I realized my attempt wasn't getting us very far.

"Okay, Pen, we're going to do a little modification," I said.

She nodded, eyes still intent on my face, as if I might whisper a secret and she was afraid she would miss it.

"Dear God ... who lives in heaven and also with us ... your name is great."

She repeated line by line, with emphasis and a big smile on "Great!"

I paraphrased some more: "We'd like for it to be like heaven here on earth … Give us what we need each day … And forgive us when we do things that are wrong … And help us forgive other people too."

Penny repeated faithfully up to that point. Then she said, "All done, Mom."

We didn't make it to avoiding temptation or to the power and the glory, but I figured she had absorbed enough. I repeated this version of the Lord's Prayer with her for the next few weeks. She never resisted, but she still looked to me for the words, and she still cut me off at some point near forgiveness. I hoped the rest would come with time.

Somewhere along the way, I gave up on teaching her structured prayer, but every so often, I remembered to invite Penny and William to pray before bed. And somehow from these sporadic attempts my kids took to praying for what they needed whenever it popped into their heads. When Penny was on her way to the hospital for a simple operation to put tubes in her ears, she prayed. When William heard that Penny was tired, he asked if we should pray. Penny's friend's mom reported that Penny stopped at the top of a slide to pray through her fear at going down alone.

My very favorite moment of unexpected prayer came when William finished the pears on his plate and asked for more. I offered him one of mine, plucked from my salad. It reached his tongue, and his whole face contorted. He spit it out, apparently offended by its coating of balsamic vinaigrette, and said, "Mom, yuck in my mouth. Please pray for me."

Prayer became a simple but reliable response to trouble, and over time I found myself a little more willing to offer my own quick requests to God, even in the most ordinary times of need. I started to follow the lead of my children. I prayed through the mundane details of my everyday life—for parking spaces and help finding my cell phone and just one night of uninterrupted sleep. I thanked God for the tulips on my desk, for my children's giggles, for the warm cup of tea in the morning.

We still prayed before bed on occasion, and one night, Penny said, "Pray. Geeka." Geeka is my grandfather, Penny's great-grandfather. We hadn't seen him in months. I complied with her request, and I prayed for him. The next morning I heard from my mother: "Geeka has shingles in his nose and throat and is in a lot of pain."

Penny asked to pray for someone apart from her usual list—Mama Dada Penny William—a few other times. Sometimes it made sense—when our babysitter broke her foot or when Penny knew a classmate had stayed home sick. But every so often she wanted to pray for someone with no reference point, and inevitably I later discovered a reason that person needed prayer, a reason Penny couldn't have known. Around the same time, I began to pay attention to my own unexpected desires to pray.

The first time it happened, I was headed down the steps, about to open the phone book to look up a place to order pizza. For some reason, I thought of our friends Elizabeth and Scott. The thought was strong, almost as if I had bumped into them in the staircase, though they lived hundreds of miles away and we didn't correspond regularly. I didn't have a sense that they were in trouble; I just felt as though they were present. I shook the impression out of my head and flipped through the Yellow

Pages. But Elizabeth and Scott came to mind throughout the day—when I put blueberries in the grocery cart, when I went on a walk, when I sang to Penny and William that night. I started to turn those moments into quick prayers, as if I were taking our friends and entrusting them to God for whatever they needed.

I finally called and left a message: "I don't know what's going on with you all, but I thought I should let you know I've had a strong sense that I should be praying for you." Elizabeth called back to tell me their son had been sick, really sick, and he had developmental delays and they didn't have a diagnosis yet. There was no question in her mind about why I might have been prompted to pray for them.

As I hung up the phone, it struck me: I had been the courier of a love letter. God wasn't paying more attention to my friends just because I was praying for them. But they had been given an outside affirmation of God's care. I, in turn, received a glimpse of heaven breaking open in the middle of the grocery store, because my daughter had given me eyes to see.

Jesus said to pay attention to the faith of children. I now try to pay attention to my children's unquestioning assumption that all should be right with the world—that pears should never taste yucky, that fear should always be comforted, and that talking to God about our problems is the most natural solution of all.

* * *

In those final weeks before the baby arrives, we make it through five nights in a row of bedtime prayers. I am still tempted to abandon the attempt again. I want to lie down on the floor and stay there until labor begins. Tonight Penny and William are poking each other and giggling and coming up with every possible diversion to delay the inevitable. "I need some ice water!" "I need to try the potty again!" "Mom and Dad, we forgot to pray!"

Despite my inner protest that I am too tired, we succumb to the last request.

William's prayer goes something like, "Mandooboo, cannal-looloo, pen!"

"William," I say, "if you aren't going to pray using real words, then don't pray at all."

He frowns at me. "May I take the laundry basket into the hallway and climb inside it?" he asks. (This is not a child who has trouble coming up with real words.) And off he goes.

Penny looks at me. "Your turn," she says.

So I pray, Peter prays, and then we turn to Penny. William has come back and now he is sitting with us, inside the laundry basket.

Penny squeezes her eyes shut, tucks in her chin, and lies down as usual. Her words are more audible tonight as she says, "Thank you for every people in our lives. Thank you for our family. And help us be kind to each other at the ballet becital." She lifts her head. "Becital?"

I meet her eye. "Recital."

"Oh, recital. And the cow jumped over the moon. And three little bears sitting on chairs." (Giggle.) "And a hat."

Peter and I share a bit of a sigh, and he says, "Penny, do you think God likes jokes?"

"Yes," she replies.

We look at each other again, and we know she is right. We all laugh.

I look forward to returning to some regularity in personal prayer after this baby is born, after sleep at night becomes more consistent for us all. In the meantime, I'm grateful that my children have given me the freedom to pray, if not continuously, then at random intervals throughout the day. In the watches of the night, when Penny has woken up with the hiccups and I sit with her hand in mine until she slides back into sleep. After a battle with William over getting dressed in the morning, with my head in my hands. During the quiet stretch on the way home from driving them to school. They have taught me that every moment, every emotion, every need, is an opportunity to pray.

I have much more to learn about prayer—not so much of methods, but of the experience of God's active presence in the mundane details of our household. I have much to learn about letting go of the shape my spiritual life took before I had children. I want to begin to receive this new life I have been given, a spiritual life in which these little ones are the central actors and teachers.

I finally start to let go of the past, to let go of the idea that prayer needs to be orderly and routinized and structured in order for God to pay attention to it. And then I begin to give thanks that prayer has burst forth from one compartment of my life and spread into the crevices of car pooling and grocery shopping and midnight trips to the potty.

One day I may offer my children more formal elements of prayer, using words like confession and supplication and thanksgiving. One day I may encourage them to write down what they pray about. One day I may even teach them all of the words to the Lord's Prayer. But through it all, I'm sure my children will continue to teach me how to pray—prostrate on the floor, giggling at the dinner table, lying in bed drifting off to sleep, but often and everywhere, talking to God.

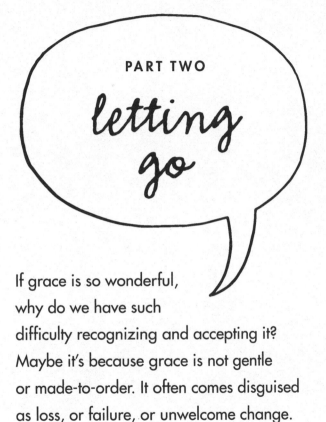

PART TWO

letting go

If grace is so wonderful,
why do we have such
difficulty recognizing and accepting it?
Maybe it's because grace is not gentle
or made-to-order. It often comes disguised
as loss, or failure, or unwelcome change.

—KATHLEEN NORRIS,
"THE GRACE OF ARIDITY AND OTHER COMEDIES"

gratitude

Maybe thankfulness is difficult because it actually is a sacrifice.

—MICHA BOYETT, *FOUND*

We are in the lobby of the ballet studio. My belly feels tight, as if the sides might split as the skin grows taut and the baby inside bumps around my womb. I am kneeling, tying Penny's shoes. Without looking up, I reach out my arm to pull William closer. The studio opens directly onto a parking lot. But now that Penny's shoes are set with her ankle braces in place, and both kids have jackets and hats and mittens, we are ready. I hoist myself up from the floor.

"Okay, guys," I say.

Penny tugs on my pants. "But, Mom, I forgot to say thank you."

I exhale somewhat dramatically through my nose. "Pen, you know you aren't supposed to wear shoes in the studio."

"Please?"

I sigh again. Class is over. Penny has received her sticker and said good-bye and we are ready to walk out the door. There is no need to thank her teacher. But I nod, because as much as it feels like an unnecessary inconvenience, I also adore this part

small talk

of my daughter. Penny loves to say thank you, and her desire to express gratitude goes well beyond adherence to parental expectations. In any class, at any restaurant, at every church service, Penny insists on finding whoever has served us and giving thanks.

I stand in place, William's hand in mine. Penny runs to the doorway and yells, "Miss Debbie!"

No response. Miss Debbie's back is turned, and Penny's voice isn't loud enough to compete with the music. Penny turns her head, looking for my permission to run across the floor in her shoes. I nod again. Soon Penny hovers near Miss Debbie, who finally notices the little girl at her side.

"Thank you," Penny says.

Miss Debbie smiles, I wave, Penny scampers back to me, and we head out.

* * *

We have a book of stories about Jesus that includes the scene from Luke's gospel where Jesus heals ten men who had leprosy. The children's version doesn't include many words, but it emphasizes that one man, just one, said thank you.

When I first read it out loud to Penny, years ago, I didn't remember this story, so I looked it up in my grown-up Bible. I read: "One of them, when he saw he was healed, came back, praising God in a loud voice. He threw himself at Jesus' feet and thanked him — and he was a Samaritan."

The other nine men probably rushed home to rejoin their families. But one returned. I wonder what was different about him, what compelled him to thank Jesus in person. Maybe it was because he was a Samaritan. Maybe, as someone from outside Jesus' own faith community, he knew he didn't deserve this Jewish rabbi's healing touch. Maybe he didn't have a family to run home to. Or maybe he was like Penny, and he just couldn't imagine walking away without saying thank you.

Penny seems to understand intuitively that she has been given much. She doesn't take her inclusion in ballet class, or the welcome she receives at our local diner, or the meal I put on the table, for granted.

But I often neglect to say thank you. I noticed it first when I stopped writing thank you notes. I got busy, but I also got tired of this perfunctory nod to social convention. Then there was the time I went away for three days, and Peter took care of the kids. He pointed out to me twenty-four hours after I returned that I had never thanked him for his work during the time I was away. I protested — I might not have said the actual words *thank you*, but that was only because I was conveying my thanks through action. Still, I knew he was right. I hadn't said thank you, and I should have. The truth was that although I told myself, and Peter, that I really was grateful, I felt entitled to the time away. In fact, it seemed hardly adequate compensation for the many days and nights I spend with our kids. Peter's words reminded me of how easily I assume I've earned every good thing in my life.

Soon after that, I was watching William in the rearview mirror as I drove. He clasped his hands together and squinted his eyes shut and said, "Thank you for my elbows!"

Elbows, dance class, a three-day vacation. I want to start acknowledging these gifts. I want to start giving thanks.

* * *

My thoughts turn to another story in the gospels that reminds me I do not deserve God's goodness, even though he lavishes it on me.

In Matthew 20, Jesus tells the story of a landowner who goes out to the marketplace one morning to hire a group of day laborers. He agrees to pay these men one denarius each for a day's work. One denarius is considered a living wage. Nothing spectacular, but exactly what the men expect to be paid, and exactly what they need in order to survive and support their families.

A few hours later, the landowner goes back to the marketplace. He hires more workers. But this time, Jesus says, he agrees to pay them "whatever is right." The landowner does this same thing throughout the day. Nine o'clock. Twelve o'clock. Three o'clock. Finally, it's five o'clock, and there are still men standing in the marketplace. They've waited ten or eleven hours, hoping for work to sustain their families. They should have given up by now. They should have gone home discouraged and hungry.

The landowner asks them, "Why have you been standing here all day long doing nothing?"

They tell him the bleak reality: "Because no one has hired us."

"You also go and work in my vineyard."

The landowner doesn't say anything about payment, but the men assume they will get an hour's worth of pay. Better than nothing.

Then the time comes to receive their wages. Instead of lining the men up in the order they were hired, the landowner tells his manager to pay them in the opposite order. He then makes a point of paying them all exactly the same amount, from the men hired last to those hired first. Of course, the men who had been hired at the beginning of the day, and who had been content to work for one denarius, complain about this turn of events.

They thought the landowner would pay them more because they had worked longer. They say to him, and I imagine their words dripped with incredulity and offense, "You have made them equal to us."

The landowner doesn't defend himself. He simply points out that he is paying them exactly what they agreed on, and he asks, "Are you envious because I am generous?"

Jesus adds one more explanatory note: "So the last will be first, and the first will be last." What strikes me about Jesus' comment is that it's only true on a superficial level. Sure, the guys who started working last got paid first. But they didn't get paid any more than the guys who started working first. The order of payment was inverted, but not the amount.

The reason this seemed like a dramatic change of course had to do with how the men perceived themselves. The people who were hired last thought of themselves as last. The unemployed. The unworthy. By paying them first, and by paying them with a recognition that they had been trying to work all day long, even if they hadn't actually been working, the landowner offers them a new self-understanding. Instead of seeing themselves as worthless, they can see themselves as valued — just as valued as the winners, the ones who got the job with the contract at the beginning of the day. Those who considered themselves last now perceive themselves as valuable, as first.

Then there are the workers who got paid last, who were hired first. Once they see that the guys who only worked an hour were paid a denarius, they do the math. Perhaps they think they'll get twelve denarii, commensurate with their twelve hours of work. They think they are the worthy ones, that they were chosen first because they really are the most deserving, the most important, the best. So when the landowner pays them one little denarius, they think they've been demoted, even though they had agreed to work for that wage. They think they have been put in last place.

The transformation for the workers in this parable happens as they see themselves for who they are — equally valuable in the eyes of the landowner. And though they were paid what they were owed, I suspect it was hard for the men who were hired first to say thank you to the landowner for what they had received.

It has taken me many years to understand that I don't deserve what I've been given. In school, I worked hard for good grades. In my first job, I stayed up late to meet deadlines. I still work diligently to make our household function and keep the kids clean and well fed. But only recently have I been able to see that work itself is a gift, a gift I have in part because of my genetic code, my family's provision of education, my white skin, and my able body. I have done very little to deserve the life I lead, yet I often see my work and family as the payment I deserve, not as a sign of God's provision. How easy it is to forget to give thanks.

* * *

Not long after Penny runs back into her ballet class to say thank you, I make a list of final preparations for the baby's arrival. I have sorted through the new toys that came in at Christmas. We have moved my desk into the bedroom and turned my study into a nursery. But we still need to bring old furniture in from the garage for the newly renovated basement. I want to find some pillows for the beat-up sofa. Through these days of prepa-ration, I have a cold. I sleep fitfully, and when I wake up, I feel the sting of helplessness behind my eyes. I cannot keep up with our household or our children. Peter has pitched in more and more—putting the kids to bed again and again, sweeping the kitchen floor, starting the laundry, getting up with William in the middle of the night and with Penny early in the morning—all in the midst of teaching classes and grading papers.

I think, *If only I had continued walking and doing yoga. If only I had been more organized or disciplined a few months back. If only I had protected my body from this cold* ... But then I remember that I'm carrying a human being inside me and I've done the best I could and we're all in this together. For a moment at least, I let go of the guilt and just give thanks.

When Marilee is born a few days later, I feel nothing but gratitude. If there is anything I could try to take credit for, I suppose it is the health of my children when they enter the world. Throughout my pregnancy, I took vitamins and abstained from certain foods and drinks and showed up for a dozen doctor's visits. I offered them the nourishment of my very self from the moment they were conceived. Yet I know I have done nothing to deserve this little one who has curled herself tight against my chest. I have not caused this soft skin and these blue eyes and this gentle, steady breathing, this health, this wholeness. I have received her, but I have not created her. She is a gift.

sin

> The handicapped [members of the body of Christ] are not primarily a problem to be solved by the rich, the comfortable and the strong. They are the bearers of a witness without which the strong are lost in their own illusions ... Their presence in the Church is the indispensable corrective of our inveterate tendency to identify the power of God with our power, the victory of God with our success.
>
> —LESSLIE NEWBIGIN,
> "NOT WHOLE WITHOUT THE HANDICAPPED"

"Babies cry to tell us something."

It has become our mantra in the months since Marilee was born. The line comes from a picture book about being a big brother, and both Penny and William have taken their elder sibling responsibilities very seriously. They happily race to procure a new diaper or item of clothing for her. They muse about how she might need to nurse when she's fussy. They try to place a pacifier in her mouth if I'm not close at hand to offer the real deal.

We've only had one unfortunate incident. I turned around when I heard Marilee shrieking and found William, wide-eyed, pointing at his baby sister in her bouncy seat. "I wanted to see what she tasted like," he said. Her arm showed an oval of teeth marks. Thankfully, he never repeated that trick.

Babies cry to tell us something.

Marilee's cries not only tell us she is cold or hungry or tired. They are also evidence of the goodness of her being, the ways in which she has been created for relationships, not for self-sufficiency. Every time she cries, she is asking me to love her.

And as I turn my energy to her needs, I begin to wonder whether my own cries, my own neediness, might be evidence that I, too, have been created for relationships. I begin to wonder whether depending on others is a part of the goodness of my being. Perhaps the areas of my life that I see as weakness are actually invitations to be loved.

* * *

Years ago, I worked as a youth minister with high school students. Every summer, a group of staff members and volunteers offered weeklong programs that included a series of talks to explain the basic story of Christianity. These talks started with the idea that God created the world and all of us, and they ended with Jesus' death and resurrection. In between, we always covered sin.

Although the teenagers in front of us might have provided good enough examples of sin from their own lives, we often went back to small children in order to defend Paul's words to the church in Rome that "all have sinned and fall short of the glory of God." We used the cries of infants and the demands of toddlers to provide concrete and irrefutable evidence of the traditional Christian doctrine of original sin, the idea that all of us exist in a state of separation and disobedience against God, from the moment we are born.

It's true, of course, that babies cry when they don't get what they want and toddlers insist on their own way. They snatch toys from one another and shout, "Mine!" They kick and hit and yell at even the suggestion that they might not receive a special treat after dinner. Tears flow with indignation at the announcement that it is time to go home from the playground or a friend's house.

But I'm not sure that childhood is the best image to present to high schoolers when talking about human selfishness. As I began to care for my own children, I also began to realize that their cries as infants were the only way they could communicate need, the only way they could call on me to feed them, to comfort them, to love them. The only way to begin building a relationship of nurture and trust with the ones responsible for their care.

I have read that one of the most distressing experiences for people visiting orphanages is the silence. Those babies have learned that their needs will not be met, so they no longer wail for attention. The silence is a mark of abandonment, of brokenness, proof only of the sin of adults who have failed to care for them.

My babies' early cries indicated their inherent yearning for relationships. Many of their cries later on told me the same thing. As my kids grew, I found myself consoling them when they spilled milk (or orange juice or water or entire platefuls of spaghetti) with words like, "You didn't do anything wrong, sweetie. You're learning. You're just learning how to drink your milk." I certainly didn't see their mistakes as evidence of selfishness or sinfulness.

It made me wonder whether Jesus spilled his milk when he was a child. Whether he cried as Mary or Joseph kissed him on the head and helped him wipe the spill from the table. Or whether, at work in his dad's shop, Jesus ever banged his thumb as he learned how to construct a piece of furniture. I assume he didn't curse and throw the hammer, but he might have sustained a bruise. Because he was human, with human limitations and vulnerabilities and needs. Like us.

I remember a time when I was pushing William and Penny in their double stroller. William asked, in his one-year-old way, to hold my watch: "Wa! Wa!" I complied absentmindedly. About three minutes later, I realized the watch was gone. I retraced our steps. I patted down their clothes. I made them get out of the stroller just to be sure it wasn't lodged underneath one of their bodies. But for all my searching, the watch — a Christmas present from Peter — was gone.

I lay in bed that night berating myself, thinking back to how I should have said no to William's request, how I should have kept an eye on the watch as he played with it, how I should have been responsible enough to avoid this loss. But I finally realized I wasn't really upset that the watch was gone. Peter wasn't mad at me. I could buy another. I was upset because I had made a mistake, and I didn't want to be someone who makes mistakes. Who demonstrates vulnerability, weakness, need. I was upset because I didn't want to be human.

A similar scene has repeated itself time after time. I make a mistake. I beat myself up. I finally see that the problem is in my desire for perfection, for self-sufficiency, not in the mistake itself.

* * *

When the doctors first told us that Penny had Down syndrome, they gave me a list of areas where she might need medical, intellectual, or therapeutic support. I saw that list as a record of everything defective, disabled, and broken about my daughter. I saw it as a list of the ways sin — working on the cellular level — had wreaked havoc within her body.

But once again, my children have shown me that my thinking was all wrong. Over time, as I watched Penny grow and learn, as I went from thinking about her as my disabled daughter to my daughter, I started to realize she was no more broken than anyone else. Sure, she had brokenness within her body, brain, and spirit. Just like her little brother and sister. Just like me. But some of what I had assumed was evidence of brokenness — a lower IQ than a typical child, a longer time learning to walk — was simply evidence that she, too, is a human being dependent on others to grow and enjoy the world.

My children's limits are more obvious than mine. William pulls his hair and mauls his eyeballs when he's tired. Penny needs the support of the railing to get down the stairs. Marilee wails without words when she wants milk. Their limitations force them to rely on Peter and me and all sorts of other people to help them out. And it is in that place — that place of giving and receiving, of needing help and offering help — that relationships are formed, that love goes forth. Limitations, properly understood, lead to love.

Whenever I start thinking I can do everything by myself, whenever I assume that mistakes here and there are the only things holding me back from perfection, I am simply playing into the pattern of Adam and Eve. I am believing I can reject my neediness and vulnerability and become like God. My desire to be self-sufficient apart from God is a sign of the sin that separates me from the love of God. In other words, it is my insistence that I can overcome my limitations that reflects my sin, not the limitations themselves.

Babies cry to tell us something.

They cry to tell us they need food and shelter and sleep and love.

In those cries I have begun to understand that we are all needy, dependent, vulnerable beings. And I have begun to believe that neediness, dependence, and vulnerability can be very good.

waiting

> Patient people dare to stay where they are. Patient living means to live actively in the present and wait there. Waiting, then, is not passive. It involves nurturing the moment, as a mother nurtures the child that is growing in her womb.
>
> —HENRI J.M. NOUWEN, *ETERNAL SEASONS*

Penny barrels into our room long before sunrise.

"I want to cuddle with you, Mom," she says. She is still wearing her footed pajamas, but otherwise she is ready for the day—glasses on, a barrette in her hair to pull back the bangs she's growing out.

"Sweetie, I just want a little more sleep."

She stays put.

"A few minutes?" I plead.

"I want to cuddle, Mom."

She climbs into our high bed and scoots her body as close to mine as she can. I pull the covers up and wrap one arm around her back. I stroke her hair with the other hand and ask, "How are you feeling, Pen?"

"A little nervous," she says. "A little nervous about surgery."

We have a long wait ahead. We won't leave for the hospital

until noon, and she can't eat anything between now and then. I don't tell Penny, but I'm a little nervous about surgery too.

We go through a pretty normal morning. Penny doesn't mind when the rest of us eat breakfast. I hear her practicing her recital dance in the hallway: "Out out in in, clap, 2–3–4 ..." Around 10:00, she asks, "May I have a snack, Mom?"

"No, sweetie, not yet."

She pinches her lips together and nods. "I know. After my surgery."

We get ready to go—pack her blanket and bear, some stickers, a bracelet a friend has sent in the mail, and several books, including *Franklin Goes to the Hospital.*

We take a trip to Target to distract her from the rumbling in her belly. Penny looks up at me and says, "I don't need to ride in the cart, Mom. I can control my hands." She selects *Dora's Ballet Adventure* to watch before surgery. And we talk through the day, over and over. "You and Dad will come with me to the hop-is-tal. When I wake up, I be a little bit sore on my eyes."

Before I can respond, a child's voice calls, "Penny!" Penny whips around and cries, "Jonathan!" when she spots her classmate. The two friends almost knock each other over with their hug.

The rest of the day goes quickly. We drive the familiar route to the hospital, wait for a bit in the reception area, wait for a bit in an examination room. Penny receives medication by mouth to make her feel sleepy. When the anesthesiologist arrives, Penny asks, "Can my mom come with me to the operating room?"

I walk next to her, clad in a white sterile getup that looks suitable for a moon landing. I ignore the equipment, the monitors, the bright lights. I give her a kiss. She says, "I'll see you in the recovery room, Mom," and then they lower a mask onto her face and she goes to sleep.

I sit in the waiting room. My daughter is lying on a table with a breathing tube as a doctor cuts the muscles in both eyes so they can regain symmetry. Another doctor will then insert tubes in both ears. Today should be one of those days when I wish she didn't have Down syndrome.

But it hasn't been a hard day. It's been a day with laughter. A day of reminders of just how lovely and loveable she is. This little girl who trusts me and doesn't complain when I tell her she can't eat. Who makes sure she hugs her brother and sister before we drive to the hospital. This little girl who loves to dance and read and who adores her friends from school. This little girl who loves to cuddle.

I think back to the resentment I used to feel at how well I knew the route to this hospital, the derision mixed with envy toward my friends who had never needed to learn about genetic counselors or child phlebotomists or developmental pediatricians. I can't even say I have let go of the resentment, more that it has disappeared, replaced by gratitude for this place, for these doctors and nurses who have devoted their lives to caring for our kids, caring for my kid.

The doctors tell me to expect five to seven days of recovery. They predict blood trickling from her eyes and significant pain. I send Marilee and William to my mother's house in case we have a truly terrible day ahead.

Penny sleeps until nine the next morning. When she awakens, her eyes look bloodshot, but she smiles, eats her breakfast, and asks, "Can we go to the playground?"

A few hours later, she is swinging from the monkey bars, happy as can be.

I watch as she giggles on the slide and scampers up the ladder. I think back on her patient acceptance as the surgery approached. I sigh with relief at her attitude. No, I marvel at her attitude. Because seeing her contentment makes it clear that I am not like Penny.

When I can't get what I want or have to do something I really don't want to do, I tend to have an adult version of a temper tantrum—only mine is directed toward God and I try to pretend I'm not behaving like a toddler. So when, for example, I have a cold or William wets his bed or Penny dillydallies instead of putting her socks on in the morning, I tend to throw an internal fit. I feel resentment churning inside me when my day doesn't go as planned. I compose mental lists to detail the ways Peter could do more to pitch in. I don't really pray, but I do lob discontented spiritual looks at heaven. I redirect my mental energy to ineffective problem solving, trying to come up with someone—a babysitter or relative or friend—who might want to take over the messy details of my life.

My attitude brings me back to the Rolling Stones song we used to sing to William when he was a toddler: "You can't always get what you wa-ant ..." It was supposed to be a humorous reminder that he could handle it when he couldn't have a cupcake for breakfast or had to eat at the table instead of having a picnic on the floor or needed to let Penny have a turn with the vacuum cleaner even though he wanted to do it RIGHT NOW. But he rarely laughed when we sang. Instead, he stomped his feet as if sprinting in place. He pushed me. He threw things. Tears shot out of his eyes like fountains.

I understand how he felt. I don't like it when things don't go my way either. I don't like to wait for things to get better. I want them the way I want them. Now.

* * *

Waiting on the Lord is a theme that runs throughout the Bible. In the Old Testament, the Israelites wait four hundred years before they are rescued from Egypt. They wait again when they are taken captive in Babylon. And then they wait centuries for the promised Messiah. Even in the midst of their immediate experience of God, they retain a constant sense of longing. They cling to the promise that someday, God's presence will be even more real and God's promised good rule will become far more evident.

Then Jesus comes on the scene, God in the flesh, the one they've been waiting for. But after he is raised to life, he leaves again. And we who follow him are called on to wait. To wait and wait and wait for his return.

It seems to me there are three kinds of waiting. There is the waiting of the Israelites in Egypt—longing, yearning for freedom and salvation. Recognizing that all is not well in the world, that we need a Savior and Redeemer to make it right. This is a discontented waiting, waiting that prompts us to demand justice now, to protest the wrongs and abuses and work to see that they never happen again.

There is also anticipatory waiting, the eager excitement that looks forward with joy to the Lord's coming, much like children look forward to Christmas morning.

Finally, there is contented waiting, waiting that hearkens back to Psalm 131, with its image of a baby held in her mother's arms, quiet, at peace. Contented waiting might also be called patience. But when things go wrong in my life—even the little things like a broken washing machine or spilled orange juice or early wake-up calls—I get stuck in a place of discontent again and again and again. Much like William protesting the lack of a cupcake, I wait with much grumbling.

When the apostle Paul writes about contentment, he says he has "learned the secret of being content." It heartens me to think that even Paul had to learn contentment. It didn't come naturally. And I'm encouraged to think that contentment is a secret. Perhaps one day I will hear a whisper from the Spirit that explains what he meant. Or perhaps the Spirit has been whispering to me all along.

* * *

The next time Penny needs tubes in her ears, I have a bad dream.

I shouldn't be worried. It is the fifth time she will be "put under," and the least frightening of the five. The previous four — ear tubes when she was five months old, a heart procedure at fourteen months, ear tubes and stints in her eyes when she was three, the ear tubes and eye surgery last year — all went off without a hitch. Her typical experience is to wake up with some degree of nausea from the anesthesia and then go back to sleep for seventeen hours.

But still I worry. She will have to make it through another day without food or drink. And by now, she remembers "that thing in my arm" (the IV). She remembers feeling scared. I will be with her through it all, but she must endure it on her own. I can't take away the hunger or the fear.

The surgery is scheduled for 2:30 on Monday afternoon. She wakes up eight hours earlier, and we repeat the familiar words that she can't eat or drink anything other than water because it might make her sick in her surgery.

"Okay, Mom," she says.

She goes to school, sipping water during snack time. I pick her up at noon. We get to the hospital, and we sit in an exam room with two books, some broken toys, and plenty of medical equipment, and we talk. We play the spelling game, where Penny gives me "hard" words to spell and then I give her "easy" ones. We talk about our visits to the hospital in years past. We talk about going out for breakfast the next day and eating an egg and cheese sandwich. She asks if she will need the thing in her arm again, and when I say yes, she nods. "Okay."

We wait and wait and wait. Penny is weak from the lack of food, so she sits quietly on my lap, and we try to find a comfortable position in a yellow plastic chair. The motion sensor lights turn off because we haven't moved in so long. We wave our hands to turn them on again. She giggles.

When the doctors finally come to get her at 4:30, she walks herself into the operating room, climbs up onto the table, and says, "Thank you" to the woman who helps her get settled. I hold her hand and talk to her as the mask goes over her face and she drifts to sleep.

* * *

When Penny was born with Down syndrome, people said she would help me learn patience. I assumed I would learn patience because it would take a long time for her to accomplish things. Books and doctors told me I would have to wait for her to talk and walk and learn her colors and use scissors.

They were right, I suppose. Penny walked when she was two, and even then she wobbled. She spoke a few words by the time she was three. But I never felt as though I was sitting around waiting for those things to happen. She was happy. She was always learning the next thing, whether it was a new sign language word or a new sound or the next motion in pulling herself up. I rarely felt impatient for her to do more or for her to do it more quickly, mainly because she seemed so content with where she was.

Penny didn't teach me about patience by forcing me to become more patient with her. She taught me by modeling patience herself.

Even when she was a preschooler, she was always willing to wait for me to figure things out.

I think back to a time when she asked me, "Where's the new shirsh?"

I wrinkled my forehead. "The new shirt?"

She shook her head, with a little smile. "No. The new shirsh."

"Skirt?"

This time, a grin. "No, Mom!" she said, in a tone of false exasperation. "The new *shirsh!*" She said the word slowly, with emphasis.

"Oh!" I said. "The new church!"

She was so proud of me.

easter

I use the G-word now — God. I feel Him holding me when I'm scared — the invisible hands I mocked years before. But this same power couldn't turn water into wine or — here's the biggie — raise the dead, could it?

—MARY KARR, *LIT*

I am trying to figure out how to explain Easter to my kids. I start with the basics: "Some people killed Jesus, so he died, and then God made him alive again."

William, at two and a half, asks, "What *died* mean?"

"Well," I say, "it's something that takes people away forever. That's why we can't see Grand Penny anymore. She died, so she is gone from this earth forever. Except when Jesus died, God made him alive again, and that's what we celebrate on Easter."

Penny looks up from where she sits paging through a picture book. She asks, "Where's Jesus now?"

I pause for a minute because I'm not entirely sure of my answer. Then I say, with confidence, "Jesus is in heaven and all around us."

She nods and says, "But where's Jesus now?"

I shrug. I don't know what else to say.

That Sunday at church, Peter and I are listening to the sermon when one of the teachers brings Penny to my side. For the rest of the service, she sits cross-legged in the black plastic chair next to me, coloring. At the coffee hour afterward, her teacher explains that they had decided to reenact the Passion of Christ in Sunday school. When Penny saw Jesus nailed to the cross, she stood up to leave.

On the car ride home I ask, "What happened in Sunday school? Did you learn something about Jesus?"

Without meeting my eye, she says, "He died. I needed to see you, Mom."

"Do you know what it meant for us when he died?"

"I don't want to talk about it."

My theological attempts at Easter aren't getting us very far, so I try another approach. A few days later, I ask William, "Do you know what Easter is all about?"

His eyes light up the way they always do when he knows the answer to a question: "Eggs! Bunnies!"

"Well," I say, "kind of."

I understand his confusion. He came home from preschool with Easter eggs. A man at our local coffee shop gave him a chocolate bunny. And we have an "Easter tree" on our kitchen table, with forsythia in bloom and painted wooden eggs dangling from the branches. I wonder if maybe I could explain Easter using these springtime symbols. We could talk about death and rebirth, about caterpillars and butterflies or chicks hatching or crocuses in bloom.

But the analogies fall apart so quickly. Nothing in the natural world is brought from death to life. What's dead stays dead. Furthermore, flowers and animals die as a part of the natural cycle of life, not because an unjust trial led to their execution. Suggesting that the cross and the empty tomb are just like the daffodils threatens to cheapen our faith and hope altogether.

Since the standard Easter symbols don't help me explain what happened to Jesus, I consider dismantling our Easter tree and forgoing egg dyeing and Easter baskets and chocolate bunnies. But Easter, for all its theological and spiritual truths, remains a celebration rooted in the physical world. I can't forget the earthiness of that weekend, the bodily death on Good Friday and the empty tomb on Easter morning. Reducing Easter to spiritual truth without physical reality is nearly as problematic as reducing it to jelly beans.

So I am left without clear answers. I am left with springtime and my children's questions about death—and what it means to come to life again.

* * *

I finally realize one reason I have trouble explaining Easter to my children is that I have trouble explaining it to myself. If I'm reading them correctly, even the New Testament writers couldn't find adequate words or images to explain what happened that weekend in Jerusalem. While the story remains straightforward—Jesus died on a cross, and God raised him from the dead—understanding the significance of that story remains a challenge.

Whenever I used to wonder about the meaning of the cross, I gave myself a stock Christian answer: "Jesus died on the cross for my sins." But over the years, I've become less and less clear on what those words mean.

First there's the problem of individuality. I don't deny that

I'm a sinner. I turn away from God through selfish actions every day. Through little things like harboring resentment toward my husband, snapping at our children, gossiping about a friend. And through bigger things like neglecting to care for people in need and participating in systems of injustice through the clothes I purchase and food I eat. Moreover, I put myself in the place of God on a regular basis. I like to decide what's right and wrong without God's guidance. I like to think I know how other people should live their lives, as if I could manage the universe with great efficiency and minimal inconvenience.

I know my sin separates me from God's goodness. Yet it seems like one more exaltation of self to think that Jesus' death comes down to my personal moral failings.

Even if Jesus did die just for me, I still wonder how the cross enabled my redemption. I always learned about the cross through analogies. For instance, I've heard humanity compared to convicted felons. So I envision myself in a line for execution, and then I think about Jesus taking my place, receiving the death penalty in my stead. The image captures the wonder of his sacrifice, but then God becomes unjust by punishing the wrong person. So then I move to a debt analogy—Jesus pays the price I owe. That captures the justice of it but misses the full impact of his sacrifice. And so on. Every time I think I understand, something pokes a hole in my reasoning.

I sometimes wonder if the same problem cropped up for the writers of the New Testament. They agree on the centrality of the cross and the resurrection of Christ. They agree that sin is a problem and we are all culpable. They agree that something happened on the cross that overcame sin and gives us access to God. But then they employ a host of metaphors to try to explain exactly what happened there. According to these early Christians, Jesus' death on the cross offers healing, forgiveness, freedom, ransom, restoration, payment of debt, satisfaction of wrath, and full life with God.

Beautiful. Hopeful. But as to how it all works—clear as the view out my window on a misty morning.

I once read about a physics concept called Heisenberg's uncertainty principle. It states that you can never measure both the location and the velocity of an electron simultaneously. Similarly, I'm not sure anyone will ever be able to pin down the exact mechanism by which Jesus' death on the cross secured my life in Christ. But I do believe that Jesus' death overcomes the power of sin both in my life and in the world around me. The cross remains a mystery to me, but it is a mystery in which I put my faith.

From the cross I move to the resurrection. Again I cannot explain the mechanism behind God raising Jesus to life. Still, from all we can tell, historically speaking, Jesus died a criminal's death, and then his followers scattered or hid. They were an oppressed and powerless group of poor Jewish men and women under Roman rule. But many, if not all, of the twelve disciples were executed because later they overcame their fears and preached that Jesus was the Christ, the King, the Son of God. Peter went from being a scared fisherman to being someone who boldly proclaimed the universal need to know Jesus personally. He claimed that the reason he preached was the resurrection.

Some Christians think the resurrection is just a metaphor for the work God can do in our lives. But I'm with Paul, who speaks for the early Christians and echoes Peter when he writes, "If

Christ has not been raised, then our preaching is useless and so is your faith." He later says that if the resurrection didn't happen, "we are of all people most to be pitied." The church has no reason to exist without the resurrection.

This group of Jews even changed their Sabbath day. For centuries upon centuries, they had kept the Sabbath on Saturday. It was a mark of distinction—of pride and of holiness, not to mention obedience to God. They observed the Sabbath the day after Jesus died. But within a few years, the Jews who worshiped Jesus were observing the Sabbath on what they now called, "the Lord's Day," which was the day of the resurrection. It's hard to imagine what else would make such a cultural shift possible.

In the same passage where he writes about the physicality of Christ's resurrection, Paul lists eyewitnesses, large groups of people who saw Jesus after he had risen from the dead. They knew as well as we do that people can't be crucified and then get up and walk around. They didn't need modern science to convince them that once you're dead, you're dead. But hundreds of people claimed to have seen Jesus, the crucified one, the one who had risen from the grave.

My rational defense of the resurrection helps me. But I'm not going to be giving a lecture about it to my children any time soon. I simply tell them that Jesus is alive, and that he is at work in the world and in my life. And if they ask how this can be, I will tell them that it, too, is a holy mystery, and yet one I know to be true.

* * *

The Sunday that Penny walks out of Sunday school happens to be Communion Sunday. Because she has excused herself from witnessing the crucifixion in her class, she unwittingly has invited herself to the Lord's Table. I don't know how much she hears when our pastor reads the story of the Last Supper. But together we walk to the front of the church. She tastes the bread dipped in juice and watches Peter and me dip ours in a chalice of wine. I don't know if she notices that we partake of these elements in front of a wooden cross. But I am glad she joins us in the practice of remembering Jesus' promises on the night before he died. She may not understand the meaning of his words, but she can act out the blessing they contain, the hope that his death gives us life.

Penny then stands on the chair next to me for the final song, raising her hands in the air and singing "My Jesus, My Savior" with gusto.

On Easter Sunday, my children will not be able to explain the meaning of death and resurrection. But we will participate together in the faith and hope that come from Jesus' gift of healing, forgiveness, and new life. We will mourn his death. We will celebrate his resurrection. And we will look forward—with jelly beans, chocolate eggs, and great hope—to his coming in glory.

listening

Whether you call on him or don't call on him, God will
be present with you.

—FREDERICK BUECHNER, *NOW AND THEN*

I think of myself as a fairly disciplined person. In high school
I wanted to improve in soccer, so I practiced five days a week
over the summer by myself. In college, I finished writing papers
before their deadlines. When I got my first job, I kept a chart of
how many hours I spent in the office and how often I exercised.
I still have the records of Penny's nursing schedule for the first
few months of her life. In other words, I like order. I like plans.
I like consistency.

But four months after Marilee is born, with Penny five and
William almost three, I have lost the rhythm to my days. Mornings that used to begin with a cup of tea and a chance to think
and pray have become opportunities to lie in bed for as long
as possible before a child demands attention. My body feels
divorced from my spirit, as if these arms and legs and breasts
are simply tools my little ones put to use all day long. I am not
unhappy, but I do feel a bit like someone spinning inside an
amusement park ride. The anchors of sleep and exercise and

consistent prayer are gone. I ask Peter for two days away, two days alone, two days to listen to God.

The first day arrives. I come up with some ground rules—no phone, no email, no internet, no television. And I come up with a schedule of spiritual reading, journaling, walks, meals, and dedicated time to listen. I pack a bag of books, snacks, and my breast pump. I walk around the corner and across the street to an empty house, a simple cottage on the Connecticut shore that has been in my family for generations. I unpack my journal and Bible, and I am ready. Or so I think.

First, it is a little chilly so I get a sweatshirt. I sit back down only to pop up again because I need a glass of water. A few minutes later, I pull out my phone to text Peter about that bill I had intended to put in the mail. I notice a voice mail from my grandmother and resist the temptation to scroll through new emails. Then, finally settled, I open my journal. I breathe in and out, slowly, meditatively, as if I am in a yoga class. I try to pray.

But instead of feeling relief at the quiet and the freedom and the time, I want to be doing jumping jacks or skipping rope. I am looking for any way to avoid a still space, a space where I have no excuse but to take a long, hard look at my life. I think of Penny in her classroom, needing to get her wiggles out before she can attend to the lesson. I decide to start the day with a walk.

I head down a familiar road, passing the cottages of families that have been connected to ours for the past century. My lungs expand as I smell the sea grass from the marsh. I trace the flight of an osprey as it clutches a fish in its talons. My heart flutters at the red-winged blackbird that intersects my path with a blaze of color beating up and down.

Walking along that dirt road helps quiet my mind. When I

return to the house, I sit on the concrete porch steps. I don't look at my watch or open my Bible. I just take in the water and the sky and the sunlight without any particular agenda. I've had a few times in my life when I heard something approaching an audible voice, a whisper of the Spirit that I couldn't explain as anything other than God's words to me, direct and clear. But that doesn't happen this time. I don't hear anything. It is peaceful, and I feel grateful, but that is it.

Yet throughout the next two days, as I continue to pick up my phone and then put it aside, as I read and journal and walk and pray, God shows up. I do not have a talk with a kindly old man with a long white beard. But I remember how it feels to be attuned to the Spirit. I ponder passages from Scripture. I take more walks and talk to God out loud and find myself at times animated, at times subdued, at times in tears. And the overriding message that comes through eternity to my temporal sphere is: SLOW DOWN.

Slow down.

Because the world does not depend on you.

Because you are beloved as you are.

Because I am God, and you are not.

Because you are a mother of three young children and they need you in particular ways. Marilee, every three hours, to nurse her and gaze into her big blue eyes and kiss her and hold her tight. William, to listen to him when he wants to talk about playing tennis with his dad and to dance with him when he requests Louis Armstrong after dinner. Penny, to snuggle on the couch and teach her how to sound out words and to tell her how proud you are when she controls her body and to receive her hugs, given with generosity and abandon.

Slow down.

At first the words come as a relief, permission to take that unsettling step off the moving walkway and stand still for a moment. But I do not know how to bring the tranquility, the beauty, the stillness, home with me. As soon as I open the door to our house, I see dishes and laundry and three needy children and the demands of work and social obligations and everything it takes to get us out the door in the morning. I never think to ask God how I might heed the admonition to slow down. And so the words fade away as my life spins along.

* * *

A few months before Marilee was born, Penny and William visited my aunt and uncle. As my aunt related later, one morning Penny refused to get dressed. She didn't cry or pout or kick. She just walked away when Aunt Jane broached the topic of taking off pajamas. Aunt Jane called Penny to come back. Penny kept walking. Finally, Aunt Jane asked, "Penny, where are your listening ears?"

Penny turned around. "I left them at home," she replied.

"Don't worry, Penny. I brought them for you," said William. He plucked them out of his pocket.

"Oh! Thanks." And from there she was set. Pj's off. Clothes on. Ready to start the day.

It didn't always go so easily.

For a time, Penny ignored our requests and commands so often that I thought she might not be able to hear us. We visited the ear, nose, and throat doctor regularly. Those mornings invariably took three to four hours and included time with an audiologist, who reported, "She's still at a mild to moderate hearing loss." But her speech was clear and she turned her head when we called and there was no reason to think she couldn't hear simple statements.

So I started to try to figure out when and why she had trouble listening. Eventually, I came up with a list. Penny didn't listen very well when she was tired. She didn't listen very well when she was distracted. But most of all, she didn't listen very well when she had her mind set on something else and my words got in the way of her desire. She didn't listen well when she didn't want to hear what I had to say.

* * *

Later that summer, a few months after my personal retreat, Peter and I are sitting across from each other at the banquette in our kitchen. The table's deep blue gloss shimmers, and I spread my hands across it, looking down. We are replaying the same conversation we have had for years, that perpetual dialogue regarding how I can have enough time to work in the midst of caring for our family and managing our household.

He says, "You're like a thoroughbred racehorse stomping at the gate. You want to run hard and fast, but the gun hasn't gone off yet."

I keep my eyes down, hearing criticism of my intensity, hearing the voices of all the women who say I should cherish each moment with these children because the rest can wait, hearing the accusation that I am not a good mother. Then he says, "I just want to figure out how to open that gate and let you run."

The tears brimming in my eyes turn from anger at the accusation to wonder at the affirmation.

But when I take the time to reflect on his words a few days

later, I hear it again: "Slow down." I don't even remember I have heard those words before. It is only when I look back in my journal that I recognize this message came the last time I stopped to listen too. A few months earlier, when I hadn't had my listening ears on.

How can I run and slow down at the same time?

I once learned that the Hebrew word for "hear" is the same word as "obey." To hear God is to obey God. If we can hear, in the fullest sense of the word, who God is, then we will obey God's commands.

But even when I hear from God the second time, I want to ignore those words. Like my daughter, I try to pretend it's not active disobedience. I'm not kicking and screaming. Just walking away. Walking away from the troubling notion that my identity is not dependent on achieving goals, accomplishing a list of things to do, providing for my children to the very best of my ability. Walking away from the unsettling idea that I should risk professional failure to serve my family for this season. Walking away, as if I can't hear. Returning to the computer and the juggling act. Perhaps the reason I don't read the Bible or journal or pray very often in the midst of the chaos has something to do with the chaos. Or perhaps it has something to do with the words I don't want to hear.

* * *

Soon Penny heads back to school. We talk every morning about being a good listener. After a few weeks, she comes home with a report card of sorts. Her teacher has divided the day into seven parts. Penny received stickers for six of them. We tape the chart to the refrigerator. She beams.

That night, I ask Penny if I can pray for her before she goes to sleep. I thank God because she's been learning how to listen, and I ask for God's help as she continues to learn. Then I say, "And Lord, please let Penny know how precious and loved she is."

We talk for a few minutes after the prayer, and then Penny looks at me. "What precious mean?" she asks.

"It means very, very special."

She nods, with a smile.

It strikes me that she has listened intently to my prayer. And in this case, listening well had nothing to do with obedience. It simply had to do with receiving the words she needed to hear: "You are precious. And deeply loved."

Penny is developing her listening ears, but I still resist using mine. The year is a whirlwind of activities, and my heart is as frantic as my schedule. I head into the following summer with grand plans of working four hours each day while my children go to camp or to the beach with a babysitter. But we start the summer with a vacation. A simple vacation, back at our family's house near the shore. With simple pleasures, like walking to the public boat launch with William and pointing out the osprey nest and marveling at his questions about mudflats and wildflowers. Dropping off the rest of the family a few towns away so they can ride a train back together. Sleeping in as Peter takes the kids out to breakfast. Visiting my grandmother. Sitting on our porch with a cup of tea and the water in the distance and praying, talking, beginning the conversation with God again. Not even noticing that I am listening. Not noticing that I am hearing words of comfort and trust. Words like "You are very, very special—precious, in fact."

Somehow this time creates in me a desire to slow down. I

suppose I finally decide to listen, to obey, but it doesn't feel like obedience. It feels as though I am receiving a blessing. And so I cut my work expectations back. Dramatically. I spend hours sitting on the beach, building sand castles for Marilee to stomp on, collecting toenail shells with William for the glass lamp we are filling at home, sitting next to Penny and counting the sailboats on the water in front of us. I find new recipes and we sing new songs and we play charades as a family for the first time.

I slow down. Not because I have suddenly become obedient out of a sense of guilt. But because I finally have my listening ears on — out of an eagerness to hear. And so I bend toward the still small voice of the Spirit, who has been whispering to me all along.

God

Any father ... must finally give his child up to the wilderness and trust to the providence of God. It seems almost a cruelty for one generation to beget another when parents can secure so little for their children, so little safety, even in the best circumstances.

Great faith is required to give the child up, trusting God to honor the parents' love for him by assuring that there will indeed be angels in that wilderness.

—MARILYNNE ROBINSON, *GILEAD*

The leaves are in their full glory. Red and yellow and crackling orange. Splashes of color against a blue sky. I push Marilee's stroller, with William and Penny on either side, as we cross the street. Peter is waiting for us. He will take the kids from here to a playground so I can go for a run.

"Hey," I say when we get closer, "how'd it go?"

"I got the job," he replies.

For a minute, I feel as though I can't breathe.

The kids don't notice. They don't know their dad has been interviewing for a new position, a move from being a teacher and coach and running a dorm to being the headmaster at a boarding school three hours away.

I manage a smile and I choke out the words: "You did? Wow." He wasn't supposed to find out until next week.

Peter smiles back. His eyes are soft, and I think he is giving me permission to delay the celebration. "I did. Go take a run. We can talk about it later."

"Congratulations," I say, swallowing hard.

I run and run and run, trying to pound the fear out of my body. But all I can think about is how afraid I am. Afraid of the work it will take to move. Afraid we won't make friends. Afraid my career will be put on hold. Afraid we won't find a church. Afraid, especially, that Penny will lose out. That in a teeny tiny town of four thousand people we won't have access to the teachers and therapists and resources she needs. That she won't make friends. That she will suffer as a result of our ambition.

I call my mom that night to tell her the news. "Oh, sweetie," she says. Her sympathetic tone is all it takes for me to cry.

Finally, later, I pray. I pray that God will take care of us. I remind God that I will blame him if it doesn't work out. I think back to all the ways God has already promised that this job is the right job, this move is the right move. And that he will be with us wherever we go.

* * *

Penny was born in Princeton, New Jersey. Though we didn't know she had Down syndrome until after she was born, we soon realized that we had inadvertently landed at what felt like the epicenter of positive experiences for a child with her condition. Our home was within an hour of the best children's hospital in the nation, with satellite specialty clinics for most of her regular checkups fifteen minutes away. Shortly after her birth, the

Special Olympics constructed their headquarters for the state of New Jersey a mile from our front door. Six other families with young children with Down syndrome lived within five miles of our house. We got together monthly. What's more, I considered Penny's elementary school the gold standard of integrated special education.

But we had always said that our dream was to settle down at a small Connecticut boarding school, so when Peter was invited to apply for the position as head of one of those schools, it seemed like the right thing. I assumed the application process would be a good experience for him. There were dozens of other highly qualified candidates in the search. We knew it was a long shot. But I also had this lurking sense that he just might get the job, and even that it might be the right job for him, for us. I started to pray, with a pit in my stomach.

I investigated the schools in the area near Peter's prospective job. They seemed fine. They didn't offer the same resources as our local schools in New Jersey, but they were well funded and they had good therapists and I knew Penny would be okay. Still, it kept me up at night.

One Saturday at dinner, two weeks before Peter's final interview, I numbered all my fears to him. They mostly centered around Penny. He offered to withdraw from the search.

I finally confessed, "I'm just so afraid. I know God has already given me reason to trust, but I need more. I need more."

The next morning, we went to church. The theme for the service, listed in the bulletin, was fear. I didn't even hear the sermon because of my swirling thoughts, but in the midst of those thoughts, it struck me, as if someone was talking to me: *God will take care of Penny, even if you make the wrong decision. Even if you mess up, God is going to be faithful to her and to you.* I felt an unexpected peace from that reminder—that as much as God had entrusted Peter and me with caring for our children, we could also trust that God would step in when we failed. I could let go of needing to get it all completely right. The God of redemption and compassion and grace would be faithful.

We came to the end of the service and the closing hymn was "Be Still, My Soul." I couldn't ignore the words of the second verse: *Be still, my soul; thy God doth undertake to guide thy future as He has the past.* I repeated it throughout the day as I thought back to story after story of God's faithfulness to me through the years. *Yes. He has guided my past, and he has guided it well. With tender, faithful care. He will guide the future in the same way.*

We went to a funeral later that day. The closing hymn was "Be Still, My Soul." Just in case I hadn't been paying attention.

* * *

When Jesus teaches his disciples about prayer, he tells them to begin by calling God their Father. Some commentators suggest that Jesus calls God by an even more intimate and personal name when he refers to God as *Abba*. "Our Father" sounds familiar now, but it may well have shocked the disciples for Jesus to teach them to call on God as if they were little children.

The Bible contains many other names for God, names that suggest God's authority—King, Judge, Lord. But Jesus refers to God as his Father, and he invites his followers to do the same. There's Jesus' story of the two sons, where we receive a portrait of an abundantly forgiving father who rejoices when his son finally begins to understand his father's love for him. There's

Jesus' story comparing God to a father whose child asks him for bread, who would never deny his child in need. The New Testament writers pick up on Jesus' words when they also, again and again, refer to this God who considers us sons and daughters.

In the eight months between the time Peter found out about his new job and the summer he actually started, I tried to trust God as my Father. But my prayers quickly turned into self-talk— *It's going to be fine. The schools are good. Everyone always says kids are resilient.* I willed myself not to worry about the road ahead. *God has made it clear that this is the right job, the right place. It will work out.*

Where we were currently living in New Jersey, Penny attended school just up the road, in an integrated classroom with two teachers and an aide who served the whole class. It was a great fit. They had enough support to handle her disruptive behaviors, and yet she was able to remain in the mix of typical kids and other kids with disabilities. By the end of that kindergarten year before we moved, she had made friends. She had also learned to read. She was ready for first grade, and I hated the thought of her in any school except that one.

But the spring before we moved, I found out that the local New Jersey elementary school only had an integrated classroom for kindergarten. If Penny were to stay there for first grade, we would need to either fight for inclusion or accept their recommendation and place her in a self-contained class. I started to feel grateful she wouldn't be at that school after all.

Then, as we were still preparing to move, I met with Penny's new teacher and principal and the special education teacher and special education coordinator for our new school district. In this small town, there was only one first-grade classroom. It came as good news that they didn't have any self-contained classes, so Penny would be integrated by necessity. Then they told me they had decided to try something new that year. Instead of having a special ed teacher visit the classroom at various points throughout the day, the special ed teacher would co-teach the class. An aide for the entire class would be there all day as well. In other words, Penny would be moving into exactly the same situation she had been in for kindergarten — two teachers, one with specific training in special education, and an aide. She would join three other children with special needs and eighteen typically developing kids.

As I walked away from the meeting Psalm 8 came to mind: "When I consider your heavens, the work of your fingers, the moon and the stars, which you have set in place, what is man that you are mindful of him, the son of man that you care for him?"

Who am I, that God is mindful of me?

* * *

We move in the summer of 2012, and soon we are living in a rental house and Peter works a lot and the kids don't sleep well. William has a tantrum nearly every day and Penny doesn't like school at first and I worry she will never have any friends. The cat loses six pounds within a month of our move and Marilee needs a shard of glass dug out of her foot and at her annual checkup Penny is diagnosed with mild scoliosis. I drink a lot of wine and eat nachos when it is dark and cold through a long snowy winter. I don't pray or read the Bible much. On the infrequent occasions when I do call out to God, I do not address him as my Father.

But almost every night, at their insistence, I sing "church songs" to my children.

Months earlier, William had asked for "Christmas church songs" instead of lullabies. That request lasted through Epiphany and beyond. Come early February, we could all recite the words to multiple verses of "Hark! The Herald Angels Sing," "Joy to the World," "Silent Night," and "O Come, All Ye Faithful."

In our new house, William changed his request. "Mom, can you sing me a *plain* church song?" A few days later, Penny, who had asked for the same songs in the same order for her entire life, said, "Mom, I want a plain church song too."

And so, in the midst of my spiritual desert, I sing. Hymns. Praise songs. African-American spirituals. Christian folk music. Liturgical chants.

Penny soaks in one song at a time until she knows all the words. I overhear her murmuring lines as she looks out the window or when we go for a walk, everything from "dip your heart in the stream of life" to "merciful and mighty" to "forever God is faithful." Her favorite song becomes "He Knows My Name," and I sing it over and over again, a reminder of what I want to believe: *Before even time began, my life was in his hand.*

When I move to William, he flops around on his bed, struggling to get comfortable, but every so often he whips his head to face me with a question. He asks, "What's the one about the guy who was lost?" ("Amazing Grace"), and, "Where is heaven on a map?" ("Be Thou My Vision"). In the middle of singing "Isaiah 40" (*Do you not know? Have you not heard? The Lord is the everlasting God* ...), he interrupts. "Mom, what lasting mean?"

I pause and look past him for a minute. "It means that God lasts forever. That God has always been there and God will always be there." I don't say it out loud, but I think, *It means that God stretches as far as we can imagine in space and time. It means that even when this moment is gone, even when the sweetness and comfort of rubbing your back and giving you hugs and kisses is over, God will be faithful. God will be with us. It means that even though I will not give God the time of day right now, God loves us. God loves me.*

He nods, satisfied. I sing some more.

And as the year goes by, in the midst of my own darkness and doubt, Penny begins to make friends. She soaks up chapter books and sets a goal for herself of doing the monkey bars. She loves school. I cannot imagine a better place for her. I feel almost bashful. I do not deserve this grace, this love, this sweetness from God.

I have many questions for a God who instructs us to call on him as our Father. I still don't understand why so many of his children don't have their needs met. I don't understand why so many suffer. But I am beginning to see that he has been my Father, night after night, singing me to sleep.

Spirit

The Holy Spirit is the power which opens eyes that are closed, hearts that are unaware and minds that shrink from too much reality.

—JOHN TAYLOR, *THE GO-BETWEEN GOD*

Once we arrive in our new town, we start attending a local church. The first week, our kids reluctantly head downstairs for Sunday school. When I retrieve them at the end of the service, Penny and William have big smiles and traces of something white smeared across their cheeks.

"Hey, there," I say, "how was Sunday school?"

"Yummy," William replies. "We had pineapples and oranges and strawberries and kiwis."

Penny says, "And whipped cream."

Their teacher interrupts with a shrug and a smile of her own. "The fruit of the Spirit never tasted so good."

I figure out that Sunday school involved a lesson on Galatians 5, but the focus of the morning, at least for our kids, is the feast of fruit. I wonder whether they learned anything other than that whipped cream is really fabulous.

Later that night, the whole family gathers outside at the table on the deck of our rental house. I am thinking through the past few weeks. We have unpacked our clothes and the kids have all started school. I can't say we are settled, but this moment is the first time in a long time that I have felt relaxed. I can hear birds chirping. The sun has started to streak the sky with bands of colorful light. The moment hints at peace that might come to our family someday, when we have found our place in this new town, this new church, among these new people.

We sing to thank God for our food, and then we hit on a familiar ritual that has been lost in these weeks of moving. We go around the table and share the high points of our day.

"Sunday school," William says.

"Whipped cream," Penny says.

"Right now," I say. I catch Peter's eye and breathe in the crisp air, the contented faces, the promise of belonging here someday.

We start to eat our grilled chicken. The kids moan about the quinoa salad.

I ignore their complaints and ask, "So, some fruit grows on trees, right?"

William glances at Penny to make sure he should be nodding.

"How would we know if that tree was a lemon tree?" I ask, pointing to an evergreen in our backyard.

They look puzzled.

"We would know it was a lemon tree if there were lemons on it," I say. "How would we know if it was an orange tree?"

William says, "If oranges came out of it?"

"You got it, sweetie! So the fruit of the Spirit, like what you talked about in Sunday school today, would be what comes out of us when we have the Holy Spirit growing inside of us."

I feel very pleased by this concrete illustration of a vague spiritual principle. Penny and William nod eagerly. Marilee throws a spoon to the floor. Peter's eyebrows are raised, as if he is slightly amused.

I have not thought about the work of the Holy Spirit in a long time. The past few months have been consumed with moving, not with prayer or theology or, well, fruitfulness. Most of the boxes are still unpacked. All of our furniture is in storage, along with a few wayward items, like our printer, that were accidentally trucked to a warehouse in New Jersey until springtime.

But tonight I am enjoying a cool breeze and a good meal and a happy family and the conversation about Sunday school. I go on. "We can know that someone is filled with the Holy Spirit when they have love, joy, peace, patience, kindness, goodness, gentleness, and self-control coming out of them." I hear the excitement in my voice as I list those admirable virtues.

Then I sigh. I look at my children's eager faces and ask, "So, what has been coming out of Mommy lately?"

Penny looks sympathetic when she says, "Screaming."

William adds, "Ungentleness."

"I'm so sorry," I say. Guilt shows up alongside the evening's lightness, as though the two might battle it out. I cannot be certain which one will win in the end, but I say, "I want to have the Holy Spirit in my life more and more. I want to be a Holy Spirit tree, with kindness and gentleness and patience coming out of me as my fruit."

Marilee throws her spoon again. The older kids nod. It all sounds so good.

* * *

Over and over again in the New Testament, the writers refer to God as "Father, Son, and Holy Spirit," but those Christians left it to the next generation to work out what exactly this triune understanding of God meant. It took quite a few years and lots of arguments, prayer, and serious study of Scripture to decide that Jesus and Jesus' Spirit deserved the same attitude, the same worship, as Jesus' Father, God. In time, the priests and scholars of the early church developed what we now call the Trinity. In fact, one of these Christian leaders, Tertullian, made up the word *trinitas* in order to try to convey this truth that God is one—utterly united and consistent in all that he is and does—and that God is three—manifesting himself in a dynamic relationship among Father, Son, and Holy Spirit throughout eternity.

Two thousand years later, it's still hard to understand. I've heard lots of analogies to try to explain this three-in-one God. I've thought about the triune God like water, steam, and ice. I've thought about God as the author of an autobiography reading out loud—simultaneously writer, character, and performer. Or like a single human being who is at the same time mother, sister, and daughter. My favorite illustration comes from a theologian, Robert Jenson, who depicts the Trinity as an infinity sign, with swooping lines. The Father sends the Son sends the Spirit. Around and up, around and up, an infinite loop of love into which we are invited.

The three persons of the Trinity are one, but it is the Spirit who enlivens the believer. God's Spirit, Jesus' Spirit, in and among us. Convicting us of sin but also comforting us in our woundedness. And, with that comfort, sending us into the world as ambassadors of love and life and healing.

My poetic sensibilities gravitate toward the Spirit, the animating force, the mysterious, beautiful, unpredictable power and grace of God here and now. Yet I still wonder how the Spirit works, what it means to walk in step with the Spirit, to hear the voice of the Spirit, to really be so connected to God that I represent God's activity in the world.

I like the fact that it took the early Christians a lot of struggle to begin to figure this out. I like the incomprehensible nature of it, the way God can't be defined. The way the Spirit is, as the Bible says, like wind, like water, like fire. Flickering. In motion. Consuming. Indescribable. One who can be experienced, perhaps, but never fully understood.

* * *

The day after my little lesson to Penny and William about becoming a Spirit tree, a new friend invites us to go apple picking. We drive down the orchard lane, and I point to the trees lining our path.

"Penny and William, how do we know it's an apple tree?"

In unison: "Because of the apples!"

I am certain they are with me in lockstep, thinking back to our conversation on the porch last night. I say, "And how do we know if we are Holy Spirit trees?"

Again, in unison: "Because of the apples!"

I shake my head with a smile.

It is a sunny afternoon. The car kicks up dirt behind us as we travel a half mile past trees heavy-laden with fruit. We are early, and my friend has said she will find us once she arrives. So we place Marilee in a red wagon and head out to the rows and rows of trees. Penny and William skip ahead, eager to fill their buckets. And I suddenly stop wanting them to understand the fruit of the Spirit. I suddenly wonder whether God designed that Sunday school lesson not so much for my kids as for me.

We walk down the rows, Marilee bumping along, Penny and William gleeful as they discover apples, as if each one is a hidden treasure even though the fruit litters the ground. The abundance astonishes me. Apples and apples and apples. We bring home three basketfuls. I don't know how we will eat them all. I have never made an apple pie. I have never cooked applesauce. Now is not the time to start. But I want all those apples around me, as reminders. And so they sit — on the counter, in a bowl in the middle of the table, in drawers in the refrigerator. We eat them with lunch and as snacks. We throw them outside for the squirrels.

A few weeks later, William asks, "So, Mom, does God move inside of us from one person to the other all the time?"

"No, sweetie. God is able to be inside all of us all the time. It's a mystery."

He sticks out his chin and his lower lip and shakes his head as if I have no idea what I'm talking about. I shrug, somewhat apologetic, but mostly content. I'm not worried that our kids don't understand a theological conundrum that has baffled and enthralled scholars, clergy, and laypeople alike for thousands of years. But I am glad William is trying to understand how the same God who created the heavens and came to live among us also lives within us and works through us. I'm glad he's thinking about God not as a cosmic rule giver or as one who looks down from above expecting his obedience. I'd rather he think about God as a mysterious but loving presence. I'd rather he glimpse the truth that only through that loving presence can we become the people we want to be.

I don't know that I understand the Spirit any more than my children do. But I have experienced a taste of that fruit in the past, and I want to experience it again. I want my children to experience it. I want them to live in a household marked by joy and peace and love. But I can't will patience and kindness any more than an apple tree can try really hard to produce peaches. So I go back to that day at the orchard and those squat, crooked trees with shiny red globes adorning their branches. I have to think that, even in the midst of this season of yelling and ungentleness, Jesus can give me his fruit. That love and goodness can come into our family, not by my hard work, but by God's grace to us. I keep the fruit bowl full of apples. I look to them as a promise.

happiness

Happiness cannot be pursued; it must ensue, and it only does so as the unintended side effect of one's personal dedication to a cause greater than oneself or as the by-product of one's surrender to a person other than oneself.

—VIKTOR E. FRANKL, *MAN'S SEARCH FOR MEANING*

Our day starts at 5:50. It is cold and dark, and I wrestle my eyes open to find William scowling, arms crossed over his chest. His forehead wrinkles into his most serious expression. "Mommy, the only thing that will make me happy is if you give me a movie right now."

I squeeze my eyes shut. "William, is it six o'clock yet?"

"No. It was taking too long."

William knows two things: he is supposed to stay in his bed until the digital clock reads 6:00, and he only gets to watch something on weekend mornings.

I also know two things: it is too early for me to get out of bed, and he will throw a fit if I don't give in. I say, "William, you can go back to your bed for ten minutes and then I will come up, or you can go start an art project by yourself."

"But Mommy! The only thing that will make me happy is a movie right now!" He emphasizes every consonant.

I try to keep my tone calm and soothing when I reply, "William, you know we've agreed that we don't watch movies in the morning."

He starts pounding the bed. Hard. Over and over and over. In the dark.

And I think, *The only thing that will make me happy is for my children to go away right now.*

By the time the tantrum is over, six o'clock has arrived. I get up. William pouts. We start another day that will be filled with what I have taken to calling ordinary-hard-stuff. William will push Penny, and a spiral will begin that inevitably ends in tears. Penny will whine about something, and I will feel the tension build within me, like heat creeping up my back. Marilee will totter across the floor like a drunken sailor and fall down and scream—whether in pain or in protest at the indignity of being a sixteen-month-old, I don't know.

At times I will feel happy today: when William breaks out into praise—"Thank you, Father!"—at the sight of apricots; when Penny suggests we pray for our cat after he vomits; when Marilee takes my hand in hers and pulls it to her cheek. But far too often, my attitude toward parenting mirrors William's attitude this morning. I am cranky because I have not gotten enough sleep and I need to provide food for five people and even the most intimate details of my life tend to involve small onlookers. I long for the day when I can take a shower without negotiating with my daughter over her wardrobe choices through the steamy glass. I think, *I will only be happy if I have finished all my errands. I will only be happy if I lose five pounds. I will only be happy if my kids will sleep until 7:00 in the morning. I will only be happy if ...*

* * *

Early on in the gospel of Matthew, Jesus addresses a large crowd. He offers a list of people who are blessed. This same word can be translated "happy," so sometimes this list, the Beatitudes, reads, "Happy are the poor in spirit ... happy are those who mourn ... happy are the meek ..." No matter how it is translated, I wonder whether the Beatitudes have something to tell me about a different kind of happiness, happiness that doesn't come from a well-organized kitchen or an idyllic reading hour with a cup of hot tea or children who are always polite, obedient, and very clean.

These verses have become so familiar that I have often thought of the Beatitudes as the scriptural equivalent of a Thomas Kinkade painting. Soothing. Gentle on the eyes. And not having all that much practical application in my daily life. But when I think about the ways I try to find blessedness, to find happiness—through control, independence, and yearning for my circumstances to change—I realize that these words of Jesus are neither innocuous nor soothing; they are an affront to my way of living.

In the Beatitudes, Jesus singles out the people we would least expect to call blessed—the poor, the meek, those who "hunger and thirst after righteousness ..." Jesus' words imply that the blessed ones don't yet have the righteousness they seek. They are spiritually earnest but destitute. They are the ones who know themselves as dependent on God. The ones who don't have it all together. The ones whose difficult circumstances might not ever change. If true happiness, as Jesus tells us, is being out of control, dependent, and needy, then parents must be one of the happiest groups of people on earth.

When Penny was four, she went through a stage when she asked me, on a regular basis, "Happy, Mom?" She usually asked after she had gotten in trouble, or after she knew she had done something well.

I almost always said, "Of course I'm happy, sweetie."

She then would ask, "Why?"

I would say, "Because I'm with you."

But there came a day when she asked, "Happy, Mom?"

"Yes, sweetie."

"Why?"

"I think you know," I said, expecting to hear the familiar "because I'm with you" in return.

Instead, she said, "Because you are loving me?"

I smiled and said, "Yes, sweetie. That's exactly right. I am happy because I am loving you."

Maybe God is naming me as a blessed one after all. One who can experience happiness in the midst of a whiny child waking me up and a vomiting cat and way too much laundry. One who can stop waiting to be happy if … One who can be happy because of the blessings implicit within the ordinary-hard-stuff. Happy because of my children's demands for my attention. Their vulnerability. The trust they have in me that I will take care of them. That I will love them well, even as I lose my temper, even as I dream about vacations and a time to come when they are older and we are more settled. Maybe I can be happy, in a new way, right here, right now.

Part of helping my children grow up is denying them the happiness they think they deserve. Maybe God, as my Father, is doing the same for me. Maybe I'm growing up right alongside my kids.

laughter

Laughter is carbonated holiness.

—ANNE LAMOTT, *PLAN B*

It is Saturday, and I am ready to go to the grocery store and leave the kids with Peter. But there is a tornado threat, so the campus where Peter works is deferring to its emergency protocols and he can't come home. It is not raining and I am not that worried about the tornado and I really need milk and eggs and fruit. So I pile all three kids into the car.

Once we arrive at the market, I manage to get William and Marilee into the store, but then I turn around and Penny is stuck outside. Maybe she isn't heavy enough to trigger the automatic door, or perhaps it is broken. Either way, she is stuck. So we walk back outside and start over and I eventually get them all in safely. By the time Marilee is situated in the cart, Penny and William have run to the snack aisle. I corral them and we go pick out two oranges, a mango, and a bag of apples. William grabs some yogurt-covered raisins. Penny drops an avocado on the floor. Marilee is trying to stand up in her seat. We have been there for approximately two minutes.

This all comes at the end of a long week that involved two

trips to the pediatrician and another round of cat pee on the bed and Penny coming home from school and announcing that she never wants to go back. My computer has crashed. A check has bounced. I cannot figure out our new health insurance plan. And the car has started to smell like rotten bananas.

So, after the avocado on the floor and the yogurt-covered raisins, I decide to abandon this mission. We leave the cart full of food in the middle of the produce aisle and climb back in the car. From the front seat, I say, "Guys, I don't know what I'm going to do. I don't know what I'm going to do. I don't know what I'm going to do." I feel as though I am stuck behind bars, pacing in my cell.

Then William says, "Mom, maybe I need to tell you a funny joke."

He makes something up about a dog that licked a lollipop, and he laughs and laughs and laughs.

And his laughter breaks through. It gets me out.

* * *

For a long time, I prayed that God would give me patience with my children. It started when William was an infant and he wouldn't sleep through the night. First I tried letting him cry it out. Forty-five minutes into that experiment, I found him as awake as ever. Three weeks later, after hours of "crying it out" every night, I decided it wasn't the responsible approach. So every night instead became a desperate prayer of, *Please, God, please let him sleep.*

Eight weeks after William was born, I had an appendectomy. Perhaps I should have counted that hospital stay as my answer to prayer. I received one blissful night of sleep before I resumed my round-the-clock nursing schedule.

There was one other night when I thought my prayer had been answered. I slept for seven uninterrupted hours. The next morning, I discovered I had mistakenly left the monitor's receiver in the playroom instead of putting it in William's room. For all I knew, William had screamed and screamed and screamed while I slumbered on to the lovely white noise of a very loud fan.

Tempting as it was, I never repeated the monitor trick. I went back to the weary and ineffective prayer that he would *sleep, please, sleep*. But he didn't. Night after night, month after month, he woke up crying.

I decided to pray for God's presence to get me through those nights. It was better than praying for God to fix the problem. But I was still woozy from exhaustion and I still snapped at Penny when she didn't respond quickly enough to my directives and I still wished for and hoped for and dreamed of more sleep. Prayer at this point seemed ineffective at best and proof of God's absence at worst.

In the midst of this long struggle, I happened to remember back to my first job out of college working for a Christian youth ministry. My boss back then told me that when things were tense at work or when she had to do something that might be tedious, like lead a staff meeting, she would pray for laughter.

I never thought I would apply that advice to my family. But then the tension that came from exhaustion filled our house and tedious logistics overtook my days. I was close to giving up on prayer altogether. Instead, I started to pray for laughter. For a long time, in fact, this was my only consistent prayer for our family.

It took all the faith I had to believe that laughter was possible in the midst of the yelling and tears and whining and discord or that it could even make a difference. But that sliver of faith remained, so day after day, week after week, year after year, I repeated, "God, please bring laughter into our home today."

Plenty of grim mornings I still found myself barking at Penny — "Get yourself in those pants right now!" Plenty of occasions — using the potty, getting dressed, putting on jackets, getting from the door to the car — still became opportunities for resentment to fester inside my chest.

But then mornings arrived when something else happened. When Penny and William were in their pajamas on our bed and I said, "After I dry my hair I think there are two little people who need to get dressed. Where are they?" and the bed exploded in giggles because Mom just asked such a funny question. Soon enough, I found myself laughing with them, and then William, convulsing, finally calmed himself down enough to sputter, "It's Penny and William who need to get dressed!" And we all laughed some more.

When William and Penny climbed into Marilee's crib and they all jostled each other and giggled about it. When Peter and I shared a bemused glance at each other after William asked, "Can you draw me an ostrich in the snow? And then a toucan?" When Penny said, "Whatever, Mom. I got it," as if she was six going on seventeen. Whenever laughter broke through, it reminded me that God was with us.

I began to appreciate how easily my kids laugh. They think unusual voices are funny, so if I talk to them as if I hailed from some exotic mixture of India, the Czech Republic, Great Britain, and Mexico, they giggle. They don't critique my terrible impersonations. They just laugh. They laugh when we make faces. They laugh when we tickle them. They laugh at nonsensical knock-knock jokes and when Peter picks them up to dance around the kitchen.

They are able to laugh, I think, because their basic needs are met. They sleep until they wake up naturally each morning. They feel safe. They know they are loved. They are not living in the future with its worries, nor are they dwelling on the past and its missed opportunities. They are living, with no small measure of joy, right now.

Jesus tells us that our faith ought to resemble that of little children. I wonder if our laughter ought to resemble theirs too. And I wonder if laughter—holy laughter, laughter that brings us together and emerges out of love—is the soil for faith.

* * *

And so, in the minivan after the disastrous trip to the grocery store, when William tells me his joke and his sisters find it hilarious, I start to laugh with them. The laughter releases the tightness inside my chest, like a potter kneading a cold ball of clay gently, firmly, until it feels pliable, responsive, ready to become something more. The laughter also leads me back to those years of prayer—when I asked, not for a pious experience in the minivan or for perfectly behaved children in the fruit aisle, but simply for moments of delight.

The laughter in that smelly car on that gray morning comes as a gift. It reminds me that God's Spirit wants to connect us to each other not just through "religious" experiences but in the midst of very ordinary, and sometimes very desperate, days. The laughter comes as an invitation to look for God's presence within our family life, no matter the circumstances. It takes me one step closer to letting go.

PART THREE

growing up

When we were children,
we used to think that when
we were grown-up we would no longer
be vulnerable. But to grow up is to accept
vulnerability ... To be alive is to be
vulnerable.

—MADELEINE L'ENGLE, *WALKING ON WATER*

love

The beginning of love is the will to let those we love be perfectly themselves, the resolution not to twist them to fit our own image. If in loving them we do not love what they are, but only their potential likeness to ourselves, then we do not love them: we only love the reflection of ourselves we find in them.

—THOMAS MERTON, *NO MAN IS AN ISLAND*

One Sunday morning, Peter lets me sleep in, and William does not approve. As the minutes wear on, he becomes more and more upset, and eventually his yelling wakes me up. As soon as I emerge from my room, Marilee takes the towel William wanted, and I refuse to override her choice. He throws a lamp to the floor, overturns the dirty-clothes basket, pushes Marilee, hurls the new towel I offer him, and then yells, loudly, for the next twelve minutes.

I have gotten a good night's sleep, so I respond to his tantrum with more poise than I typically would. I hold him until he calms down, walk him through apologies to the rest of the family, and then sit down with him to snuggle.

"How much do I love you?" I ask.

William shrugs, a little worried he might give the wrong answer.

I hold my index finger and thumb a few inches apart. "This much?"

He looks perplexed, shakes his head slightly.

I put my hands about a foot apart. "This much?"

His eyes light up, hoping he knows what's coming, and he shakes his head again.

I stretch my arms out as wide as I can. "This much?"

He nods vigorously, confident at last, but I say, "Nope. I love you longer than my arms can reach," and I give him a hug.

As I hold him close, his silky hair tickling my chin, his plaintive brown eyes closed for a moment, his strong, skinny limbs tucked into my lap, I feel a surge of affection for this boy of mine. It's a sensation that usually comes when I stand in the doorway and gaze in on him or his sisters asleep, when I try to memorize those features at rest, when I take the peacefulness of their bodies into my own and my heart rate falls and my breathing becomes steady and slow. It's a feeling of warmth and wholeness, like lying on a raft in the middle of a lake on a sunny day. It's a feeling of permanence, even though I know that as soon as a cloud covers the sun I will shiver again and dive back into the chilly water and the warmth will become a memory.

With my arms around him, I think back through the years of hugs and playtime and singing him to sleep. When William was born, I didn't feel love for him much of the time, at least not in the airbrushed Gerber baby ad kind of way. Idyllic moments came every so often—when he nursed and cooed, milk dribbling out of the corner of his mouth, when he looked up and his eyes locked onto mine, when he grabbed my index finger and held on tight. But more overwhelming were the diapers and the wriggling and kicking and the wailing in the middle of the night. My love back then came through my body. My aching back and bleary eyes stood as reminders of the physicality of my devotion to him. Even when he wasn't in my arms, I found myself rocking from side to side.

I had experienced that same type of tangible love two times before—once when Peter's mom, Grand Penny, was sick with liver cancer, and again after our own Penny was born. In each case I found myself wishing I could walk away from the mess of it all. The poop and spit-up and blood. The vulnerable bodies demanding attention and care. I wished I could walk back to my life the way it had been before, when it was just Peter and me in our own relatively blissful existence, with one cat and a tidy little house with walls we had painted ourselves. I wished I could return to a life without tears or pain or chaos.

But I didn't walk away, at least not forever. And in returning—to my mother-in-law, to my children—I learned to love them.

When Marilee was born, two and a half years after William, I discovered I had grown accustomed to love's demands on my body. She slept more easily than her older brother had, and even as an infant she seemed content to simply watch the world and respond with a smile. Putting on a new diaper was no longer an act of fumbling concentration, as it had been with Penny. Getting her to sleep did not require hours of arduous bouncing and rocking and desperate prayers, as it had with William. Caring for her still required my touch—bathing, feeding, stumbling into her nursery in the middle of the night—but it didn't exhaust me in quite the same way it had with her siblings.

The temptation with Marilee was to distance myself from her needs even as I went through the motions of fulfilling them—to let her cry a few minutes longer so I could finish a project, to read an article on my phone while she nursed, to create a to-do list in my head as I wiped her or bathed her or changed her clothes. Marilee was easy, so I had to remind myself that paying attention to her was not a task to accomplish. Denying my impulse to be productive and instead cooing at her, studying her features—the dimple in her chin, the rosy cheeks, the wispy black hair—and letting her rest against me, body to body, warmth to warmth, would somehow build a foundation of care for years to come.

* * *

As I hold William close, I think about how the physical acts led, ultimately, to the emotional response—to the gradual expansion of love, from a love contained between an index finger and thumb to one that spread out wider than I could ever have imagined.

William starts to shift his weight, and I know the moment is over. He sits across from me on the bed, his eyes cast down.

"William, I need you to clean up everything you threw on the ground earlier," I say. "But first I need to tell you one more thing. Even when you wake me up and yell and scream, I love you."

He doesn't move.

"Even when you throw lamps and towels and dirty clothes, I love you."

He nods.

"Even when I yell back at you and get mad, I love you."

He looks up at me.

"Wider than my arms can reach."

* * *

When I first read that classic biblical equation "God is love," it appeared to be a simple, even sentimental, statement of fact. The famous passage from 1 Corinthians 13 seemed equally happy and rudimentary. *Love is patient and kind and keeps no record of wrongs.* It sounded nice and easy and attainable.

But as I discovered what it took to love my children, these sentimental ideas of love floated out the window. The hard work of love took their place.

I eventually learned that the Greek language has words for different types of love that all get translated the same way in English. There's *philia*, brotherly love; and *eros*, erotic love; and *storge*, natural affection. Apparently the Greeks used *storge* most often to describe the love of a parent for a child, but I guess I'm not like the Greeks. I've found that natural affection for my children arises mostly when I am watching them from a distance or when I have a rare special time alone with one of them or on a lazy Sunday when we all go to a playground together. Day in and day out—amidst packing lunch boxes and making sure Penny and William don't get into a fistfight and keeping up with their sixty toenails and fingernails and negotiating turns on the iPad—natural affection is often in short supply.

But when in the Bible John writes, "God is love," he uses the word *agape*. God isn't *storge*, natural affection. God isn't friendship or romance, *philia* or *eros*. God is sacrificial love, a love that gives everything. And although *storge* is used more often, apparently the Greeks used *agape* to describe the relationship between parent and child too.

Love for my children may begin and even end with sentiment, with *storge*, but the middle place of patience and dirt and sweat and kindness and feverish bodies and wet beds and perseverance and dirty laundry and broken dishes — the middle place is filled with action and hard work. With *agape*. With something that comes from God and returns us to God.

* * *

I lean over and kiss William on the forehead. He moves slowly off the bed, sliding to the floor with a thump. He starts to put the clothes back into the hamper. I join him, and we work side by side for a few moments. Once we finish, he races off to find his sisters, and soon enough he and Marilee have raided my closet. They emerge with leather boots up to the tops of their thighs. He wears a pink scarf, a red hat, and a sequined top. Marilee has discovered one of my long cardigans, complete with faux pearls, and a black shopping bag to serve as a purse. Penny, who has never much liked dressing up, sits on our bed, reading *The Trumpet of the Swan* out loud to herself.

"We goin' a wesawant, Mommy," Marilee announces. "We havin' a date."

She and William tromp out of the room, mimicking their mother and father, who routinely go out to dinner on Thursday nights. All is well. Anger abated, dispute forgotten. I start to get myself ready for church.

As I go through my own routine, I think about all the ways our kids try to act like us. I smile at the memory of Penny brushing her teeth, age four, with a *Time* magazine in one hand. She was pretending to read an article while preparing herself for the day, just like her mom did. I think of William, who loves to sit in front of a computer and "type" as quickly as he can, so he can do work like his dad. Marilee imitates her big brother and sister as much as she does her parents, insisting she can sit in a big-girl seat and go down the superhigh slide and run and skip and climb, even if it results in shins painted with bruises.

Some of this imitation is natural human development, of course, but I suspect it also has to do with love. It makes me think again of a verse from the Bible, this time from Ephesians: "Be imitators of God, therefore, as dearly loved children, and live a life of love, just as Christ loved us and gave himself up for us as a fragrant offering and sacrifice to God."

At first it strikes me as an impossible command. How on earth would we imitate a limitless, omniscient, omnipotent being? But there it is again, that call to *agape*, that call to love sacrificially. The verse is lathered in love. Dearly loved children. Living a life of love. Just as Christ loved us. *Agape, agape, agape.* Just as my children imitate me, I have been invited to imitate God in this way of sacrificial love.

The truth is, *storge* runs its course fairly quickly. When natural affection is gone, I can either walk away or I can lay down my needs and wants for the sake of my children and love them with *agape* love. Because God loves me this way. Because he has already stretched his arms as wide as they could reach.

I watch Marilee and William traipse out of the room in their "clonk-clonks" (any shoes that make a terrific racket on hard-wood floors), and I begin to think that this impossible command to imitate God is really an invitation to intimacy—even to the particular intimacy of a child with a parent. The intimacy of Marilee asking me to brush her nose with powder as I put on makeup. Of William standing next to me while I wash my face, just to have his body close to mine. Of Penny starting each morning with a smile and a hug and a request to cuddle for a minute. The intimacy of my children asking me for what they need without apology because they assume that my affection and care for them will last forever, no matter what they do. The intimacy that has room for anger and sadness and laziness and mistakes. The intimacy that emerges from those early days and weeks of physical care and grows into affection and continues to build toward reciprocity, toward a relationship of giving and receiving. The intimacy that assumes *agape*, a love that never fails.

Peter and I eventually coax William and Marilee out of their dress-up clothes and into church outfits. Penny puts down her book. I dry my hair. We head out together. William reaches for my hand as we walk down the aisle to claim our spot in the first pew, where he can watch the organist play and the whole congregation can watch us attempt to keep our wrigglers still.

The service progresses. Marilee ends up in the nursery long before the children's message begins. Penny tries to sing along with the hymns. William breaks two pencils as he colors a drawing of Jesus and the miraculous catch of fish.

And all I can think about during the service is how much I am like my son. How much I resist God's grace and God's guidance. How often I insist on my own way and make a mess in the process. How often my to-do list gets in the way of being still. How instinctive it is to think that God will respond by giving up on me.

When what God really does, over and over again, is love me.

Throughout the prayers of the people and the Scripture reading and the choir's anthem that morning comes yet another whisper: "How much do I love you?"

Finger and thumb an inch apart. "This much?"

Hands about a foot from each other. "This much?"

Arms stretched wide.

miracles

> We modern people think of miracles as the suspension of the natural order, but Jesus meant them to be the restoration of the natural order. The Bible tells us that God did not originally make the world to have disease, hunger, and death in it ... Jesus' miracles are not just a challenge to our minds, but a promise to our hearts, that the world we all want is coming.
>
> —TIMOTHY KELLER, *THE REASON FOR GOD*

William and I are on the couch together, watching *The Prince of Egypt*. An animated Moses stands in front of the Red Sea with the frightened Israelites, wondering how they will ever escape the wrath of the Egyptians. William's whole body sits at attention—spine straight, eyes wide—as Moses looks out at the water.

Disney portrays the event as faithfully as I would expect it to—the sea parts and two walls of water rise up on either side. It's still not an easy crossing—carts break, babies cry, fear of both the Egyptians and the water remains. But the Israelites make it across, and then the water covers the sea floor again. It is an awful, awesome depiction of an awful, awesome event.

When it is all over, William asks, "Mom, how did that happen?" He snuggles against my body now, his head resting on my chest.

"It's called a miracle," I say. "It happens when God decides to do something that humans can't do all by themselves."

I feel his head nod. But then he pushes himself up and looks at me. "But did it really happen or was it pretend?"

I pause and meet his gaze, offering a barely audible sigh to my little boy who turned four only a few months back. I say, "Well, the Bible says it happened."

I think for a minute about how much I want to try to explain my own faith and doubt, my own questions of what this story is all about. I finally say, "It's a story that tells us about how much God loves his people and how he will always help them and rescue them."

That satisfies him for the time being, but I suspect this son of mine, who has inherited his mother's rational mind, is not done wondering about miracles.

Neither is his mother.

* * *

When the time comes, I will try to tell my kids more about what I believe. I will explain that I always start with what I know to be true about God. I will explain that we know about God first and foremost through Jesus. And we know about Jesus through what the Bible tells us.

One day, I will tell them that different parts of the Bible are written differently. Maybe I will pull out a cookbook and a poem about food, and we will compare and contrast these two genres. We will note together how the cookbook gives specific instructions, with little room for interpretation or ambiguity. We will note how the poem, even if devoted to the same subject matter, is trying to tell us something very different, something about the experience of eating, something about being human.

I will explain that the Bible contains poetry and history and stories, that each part of the Bible has to be taken on its own terms, that the poetic passages and the historical passages are different from one another and we need to respect their differences. I hope this approach will help us with some of the texts that prompt questions.

I think I understand how to approach biblical history and biblical poetry. The problem is that I don't know how we are supposed to read the stories, the narratives that fall in between history and fable, in between fact and fiction.

From what I understand, the Israelites read their stories differently than I might as a twenty-first-century American. Some of them—Jonah, Job, even the early accounts in Genesis—offer context clues to suggest their purpose is not so much to record historical events as it is to tell a true story about God's nature. Other Old Testament texts provide details linking them firmly to the historical record of the Jews exiled to Babylon. Then there are the stories in Exodus, foundational stories for the Jewish faith and for my faith as a Christian. I'm less clear on whether to read these stories as historical narratives or as tales of God's redemptive goodness that don't accord perfectly with the historical record. As someone trying to read these texts faithfully, I don't know what to make of it all.

So one day I will tell my kids that I'm not sure what to believe about the parting of the Red Sea and Noah's ark and the battle of Jericho. I will tell them that it is unclear to me how I am supposed to read Exodus. As God's Word, yes. True for the

Israelites and true for us. But also as a story from a people who told stories, from a culture where the purpose of the story was truth about YHWH, perhaps more than the facts about deliverance as it happened in real time and space.

I will also explain to my children why I believe in the foundational miracle of the resurrection. I will explain that I believe it is a physical reality and not just a spiritual hope, that Jesus rose from the dead.

I will talk about how the gospel stories cry out for the eyewitness validation that others provided. I will talk about the men and women who gave their lives because they believed in what they had seen—Jesus, alive again.

And I will tell them my story. How God has answered prayers, small and large. How I know people who have experienced inexplicable healing. How I know people who had visions that came true. How I believe reports from missionaries that, even today, the sick are healed, the lame walk, the blind see. That, even today, God is good and loving and ready to intervene in our brokenness.

In telling my children all of this, perhaps I will convince myself of the Exodus miracles too. That a God who can raise the dead can also part the waters of the sea.

* * *

On the night after we watch *The Prince of Egypt*, I sit down to sing to William before he falls asleep. I say, "You know, that song from Isaiah 43 talks about what we saw in the movie today."

"Will you sing it for me?"

When you pass through the waters, I will be with you, and the wind and the waves will not overcome you. Do not fear . . .

"It's a song you can sing if you're ever afraid," I say. "To remind you that God is always with you."

He nods, my brown-eyed boy with those long eyelashes and dimples, too old to be sucking the pacifier in his mouth, too young to be working through the mysteries of the cosmos.

"I can also sing it if I'm sad," he says, "because God will be with me then too."

I rub his back, running my fingernails lightly against the smooth skin as his eyes close and he drifts off to sleep. If there is anything I want him to know with certainty, it is this—the constant presence of a loving God who will be faithful to him in the midst of doubts and fears and questions and wandering. A God who will be present even if he should one day turn his back on everything he has been taught to believe. A God who will, as he did with the Israelites, always be working to carry him home.

For months after that moment, William asks for the "water song." And every night I sing this song that reminds him, reminds me, of the miraculous love of an ever-faithful God.

tragedy

Friend, in the desolate hour, when your soul is
    enshrouded in darkness,
When in a deep abyss memory and sense disappear,
Intellect timidly gropes among shadowy forms and
    illusions,
Heart is unable to sigh, eye can no longer shed tears;
When from your night-clouded soul the wings of fire have
    fallen,
And you feel yourself sink, fearful, to nothing once more,
Say, who rescues you then? . . .

—ERIK JOHAN STAGNELIUS,
"FRIEND, IN THE DESOLATE HOUR"
(TRANSLATED BY BILL COYLE)

*Just saw a headline about a shooting at a school in Newtown,
CT, not far from you. Hope all is well.*

A text from my brother-in-law alerts me to the news. A quick
internet search yields information about a teacher wounded at a
school in western Connecticut. I text back: *Oh gosh. We are fine
but that's scary—looks like an elementary school too.*

I close my computer and meet a friend for lunch. It is a beautiful day. The sky so blue. The air like a drink of cold water.

A few hours later, I read an email from Penny's principal.

Her school is in lockdown. I check the news again. A young man has forced his way into Sandy Hook Elementary School, twenty miles away. He has murdered twenty students and six adults inside the building before taking his own life.

It is December 14. Four hours from now, our family is due to light the town Christmas tree. The night should be merry. The shops will stay open late, offering cookies and popcorn and balloons and prizes for kids. Carolers will perform on the lawn of the town hall. Santa will hold children on his lap and all the kids will line up for a horse-drawn carriage ride. I call Peter and say we shouldn't go.

But the day rushes on and we never have time to talk about whether we should still show up, and so we drive down the hill into town. The children run in circles around the old fir tree once it shines with light. They giggle and chase each other and cheer when Santa arrives. The adults choke back tears. I push the sadness from my throat into my chest and walk from store to store, fixing Marilee's hat, promising Penny she doesn't need to see Santa if she doesn't want to, helping William reconstruct his balloon sword.

We don't read a story before putting the children to bed that night, but William asks me to sing "O Come, O Come, Emmanuel," as he has almost every night for two weeks running. I sing with a sense of gratitude for the haunted melody, the minor key that begs Jesus to come back. As if it might really happen one day—the joy and promises and glad tidings. As if we must cling with all our might to the shred of hope that one day every tear will be wiped from our eyes. *Rejoice!* the song commands, and yet the music gives permission to mourn, to stand in the anguished place between the promise and the pain.

* * *

Once the children are asleep, I pore over the news reports, as if more information can dilute the horror. But it only gets worse. I learn that the shooter killed his own mother, then at 9:30 on that bright sunny morning, he gunned down those twenty children and six adults at the school. The children who died were all in first grade. Six and seven years old. Just like Penny.

I think of her classroom—of George and Emma and Victoria and Julian. I think of the ways the children are just starting to grow up, just starting to be a little bit mean to each other, just starting to know how to be kind to one another. I think of Landon's white-blonde hair. Of the way Lily wants my approval when I volunteer in the classroom. Of how Joshua pouts when he doesn't get his way. I think of their earnestness—that Callie or Sophia always tells me when Penny hasn't been keeping her hands to herself at lunch. I think of the lightness to their bodies, the way they jump up from their seats and cozy into the beanbag chair in the reading corner and prop their elbows on their knees, sitting cross-legged on the carpet squares.

We keep the television off all weekend, and our children don't seem to notice when adults huddle in corners and whisper to each other. We go to ballet, to a puppet show, to a birthday party. We go to church, and our pastor opens the service with a declaration that gathering to worship is an act of defiance against the violence, a refusal to acknowledge the darkness, a decision to continue to hope. I hold a squirming Marilee on my lap and suppress a cry. I am not sure. I am not sure that the darkness has not won.

The kids perform their Christmas show that morning.

William tells the congregation that Jesus was born in a stable. Penny declares that we celebrate Christmas because Jesus was born. They sing "Away in a Manger" and "Silent Night." Marilee sneaks up to the altar to ring one of the bells from the older kids' bell choir. Then they go downstairs, and our pastor offers the adults a time to question God, to cry out, even to shake our fists at the heavens.

I am not so courageous. I offer a prayer out loud for the families, and I end my prayer with words of hope. Perhaps I do not need to stay in the darkness, because it was not one of my children who died. Perhaps my faith is so strong I will always hold on to hope. Or perhaps I cannot stand the thought that darkness might have triumphed and I have to pray as if it has not—if only to try to convince myself. After the service, we eat cookies and drink punch and sing the doxology in the church basement.

That evening, I pull Penny onto my lap and say, "Penny, something sad happened to some kids." I tell myself I am telling her because she might hear about it at school and I want her to be prepared. But I wonder if I need to tell her because I need to know that it didn't hurt her, that she is okay.

She studies my face, as if reading it for clues. "Who?" She tilts her chin up, and I feel the softness of her hand in mine, the warmth of her body. I see the concern behind her big green eyes.

"It wasn't anyone you know," I say. "But kids got hurt and it was sad and scary. If you have any questions or hear about it at school, please come talk to us or to another grown-up." My voice cracks and the tears roll down my cheeks.

Penny opens her arms wide and hugs me. "Can you read me a book?" she asks.

But my tears keep coming. Penny puts her arms around me until I say, "It's enough," and start to push her hands away.

"I was just tryin' to make you feel better," she whispers.

And the pain that has spread throughout my chest all week-end seems to locate itself within my heart.

* * *

I volunteer in Penny's classroom on Monday. *This is what a school should be*, I think as I walk through the building. *A safe, happy, colorful place, where it doesn't cross kids' minds to be afraid.*

I enter the rambunctious cheer of her classroom. The students are working to create a wreath out of puzzle pieces in anticipation of the upcoming holiday. As I supervise gluing and coloring, the thoughts keep coming, unbidden, of the kids who won't take wreaths home to their parents this year.

I am working with a group of students when one of Penny's classmates, a little girl who also has special needs, walks past the table with her classroom aide. I have never heard Laura speak more than one word at a time, but I have noted her gentle smile, her kind eyes. I learn later that two of the children at Sandy Hook who died had autism. I learn later that one of them was found underneath his aide, and I hope that her love for him was all he knew as the bullets pierced his body.

One of the boys at my table, Joshua, labors to write his name as he says with a raised eyebrow, "Laura does what Laura does."

I say, "And I'm sure Joshua does what Joshua does too."

He looks up from his work. "I'm smarter than she is," he says, as if I had misunderstood him the first time around.

"I'm sure there are many things you are good at, and many

things Laura is good at too," I say, but he has turned his attention back to his work.

A few minutes later, I notice that Joshua is in the reading group that is learning how to sound out words, whereas Penny is in the one discussing chapter books and learning vocabulary words like "wended." I catch myself wanting to say to him, *Well, Penny is smarter than you are.*

And I think about the nature of evil, how it can seem so benign to think I matter more or that my child is better, how it is so easy to turn away from kindness.

Later that week, Penny and I are returning from an appointment with the ear doctor. We drive through a little town, with its sleepy main street and wreaths adorning clapboard houses and businesses, and I see orange cones and police cars and a mass of black sweaters and overcoats and hats. And a sign, "Pray for Newtown." It is a funeral for one of the teachers. Penny says, "Mom, why are you crying?"

I gulp and take a deep breath and say, "You remember how I told you about some children who got hurt at a school?"

She nods.

"Well, some of the kids who got hurt died, and some of their teachers died."

"But no one we know."

"Right," I nod, biting the inside of my lip. "But it's still sad, sweetie, to think that there are some kids and teachers who died."

I cannot explain empathy to her. I cannot even explain it to myself. Somehow the physical proximity to this crime has made it more troubling than the other shootings that happened this year. The fact that they were first graders, just like her. The fact that two of the children had special needs, just like Penny and Laura. I can imagine this horror in a way that I cannot imagine war or gang violence or other things I read about in the news. It hurts more, this ache of guilt and gratitude.

* * *

We abandon our Advent calendar on December 14. It isn't an intentional decision. We never declare that we cannot hold out the hopeful anticipation of the Christ child this year. We get busy. We need to buy presents and pack to go to my parents' house and send out the Christmas cards and find someone to feed the cat.

One week after the shootings, I pick Penny up from school.

"Why there are police?" she asks, as she holds my hand and skips to the car. She slows down, taking in the vehicles. It is drizzling. "Mom, there are two polices."

"Yes, sweetie. You remember how those kids got hurt? The police are here now to make sure you stay safe." I squeeze her hand, and I wonder if I am lying. For I know that I cannot, and the police cannot, make sure she stays safe. Sandy Hook Elementary had plenty of safety precautions in place. The teachers acted with sacrificial love. The blood of children was shed anyway.

I keep praying that God will undo it. That we won't have to wait for all the horrible things in this world to be redeemed. That those children will come back to life right now. But my prayer is not answered. The final funerals have taken place, and there are two police cars in the bus line at my daughter's school.

Penny says, "Why would someone hurt those kids?"

Penny's classroom aide sees her before I can answer. Mrs. G.

opens her arms wide. "Penny! I have to give you a hug before you go on vacation!"

Penny runs, her legs akimbo, her backpack bouncing, to offer one last embrace.

I think back to the moment I first learned about evil in the world. I was driving with my mother — back in the days when children were allowed to sit in the front seat — and I must have been about eight years old. We had a yellow Volvo with a black leather interior. The seat stuck to my body in the summer, even if the air conditioner was on. But it must have been winter, because I remember the gray in the sky and the outlines of trees poking up from the ground. I don't know where we were going or how it came up, but I know we were driving along a desolate stretch of road when I asked about the Holocaust. Mom told me about Hitler and the gas chambers and the millions of people who died.

On that day I wanted my mother to stop the car. I wanted to stand on the side of the road and scream or vomit or pound the earth with my fists. But I held the horror inside and asked a few more questions and I tried to understand hatred.

I do not want Penny to ever be able to understand why someone would want to hurt a child. I do not want her to ever have any reason to ask the questions she is asking.

The next day, Penny is out Christmas shopping with my sister Elly, and they hear a siren. "Elly, those are ambulances," Penny says. "They take people to the hospital when they need a surgery." Then she says, "Some children got killed."

"Yeah, I know, Pen," Elly says. "It's really sad."

Penny asks, "Why?" and Elly doesn't know if Penny wants to know why the children were killed or why it is sad, but either way she says, "I don't know, Pen. I don't know."

On Sunday morning we sit in church as a family. William cranes his neck to see the trumpet. Penny complains that the music is too loud, so Peter takes her into the hallway for a while.

"Some children died," she says.

"I know," he replies.

"Did they go to heaven?" she asks.

"Yes," he says without hesitation.

"Then why is it sad?"

He has to look away for just a moment as he tries to explain. "You know how Grand Penny died and went to heaven? Well, we are happy for Grand Penny that she gets to be in heaven, but we are also sad that she can't be here to give us hugs. And the parents of those kids are sad that they don't get to give them hugs anymore."

Penny nods and is silent. Christmas Eve arrives, and we sit in a circle with my extended family — my grandparents, their four children, my three sisters and five of our cousins, my three children and two nephews. Someone starts to sing. Most of my family has abandoned church, but somehow even the ones who haven't set foot in a sanctuary in years come up with the words to the Christmas hymns.

Penny and William have been asking me to sing these songs before bed the whole year, so they join in with confidence. We sing three verses of "Joy to the World." We proclaim the *wonders of his love.* We sing of *God and sinners reconciled.* We sing, *Sleep in heavenly peace.*

That night, as we have for years, we have a birthday party for Jesus with a cake and a few presents and a song. This year, Penny reads a children's version of the Christmas story out loud all by herself while William places the pieces of the Nativity scene on the coffee table in the living room. He constructs a perch for the angel out of a Fisher Price town and two throw pillows. He makes room for the camel and the sheep and the wise men. He lets Marilee place baby Jesus at the center.

Penny doesn't ask again about the children or the teachers or the funerals or the police. The pain in my chest slowly dissipates. But the questions she asked— *Why would someone hurt those kids? Are they in heaven? Why are we all so sad?* —and the questions she didn't ask— *Where was God as the bullets flew? Couldn't God have stopped it? Why is there so much sadness in this world?* —never fade. The questions, and the sorrow, and the hope of the baby in the manger, remain.

kindness

> The fondness, the endearment, the unstintingly affectionate regard of God toward all his creatures is the natural outflow of what he is to the core — which we vainly try to capture with our tired but indispensable old word "love."
>
> —DALLAS WILLARD, *THE DIVINE CONSPIRACY*

At first when I hear William singing, I think he is showering his sister with affection. "I love you, Marilee. Marilee, I love you."

But then I see the scowl on her face and the smirk on his, and I realize that his words are intended as a taunt.

She soon responds, singing over him, "I do not love you, William. William, I do not love you."

Before too long Penny has joined them at the breakfast table, and the usual squabble begins.

Marilee shouts, "Mama! Penny's feet!"

I look over. Penny's face remains blank, as if she has no idea why Marilee would level such a slanderous accusation. But underneath the table I see her foot sliding over to Marilee's chair and darting back again. And again.

"Guys, you keep your feet in your own space or you sit by

yourself. You know this." I raise my eyebrows at Penny until her blank stare becomes a contrite nod.

I have become used to the role of referee. Much of the past five years—since William came into the world and competition for parental affection became a daily aspect of family life—has been dedicated to managing these types of behaviors. Every day, every single day, involves disputes. Wanting what someone else has. Protesting unfairness. Hitting each other instead of talking it out. "Don't grab!" has been an almost constant refrain. Added to it: "Mom, William hit me!" "Marilee, that's mine!" "Penny won't listen to me!"

Occasionally I see something other than petty disputes and self-centered desires. When Penny needs to get a new shirt from upstairs and Marilee volunteers to accompany her, "so she won't be alonely." When Penny falls and starts to cry and William sprints to get the bear she sleeps with at night. When Penny offers to hold Marilee's hand because she has an ear infection and feels a little bit nervous about the antibiotic drops trickling into her ear.

As I think back on it, care for one another has been there all along, right alongside the selfishness and shouting. Even when they were little, Penny gave William a kiss if he got hurt. They held hands in the backseat of our car. She was the first person he asked for when he woke up in the morning.

I remember one time when William was still skittish about loud noises. He must have been about to turn two. He and Penny and I were in the kitchen. I pulled out the blender and put blueberries and yogurt and a banana inside.

William looked at Penny. "Loud?" he asked.

"Medium loud," Penny said. "I will hold your hand."

They shuffled away from the blender together, until their backs ran into a cupboard. When the noise began, William's eyes got wide, but they didn't spill over. Penny hugged him the whole time.

I turned it off, and she said, "See, William. I will keep you safe."

Now the three kids bicker and yell, and they also compromise and look out for each other and laugh together. Two instincts compete within them — the instinct to love and the instinct to protect themselves at all cost. I want to nurture that first instinct. I want to teach them to be kind.

* * *

I always thought of myself as a kind person. I was the kid who looked out for the ones on the fringes. One time in middle school, I sat with a girl who was by herself at a table in the cafeteria. She had stringy hair that was a shade between gray and brown. She was pudgy, and her eyes weren't quite straight. And I remember thinking, with a sense of self-satisfaction, that it would be nice of me to sit with her.

I recall nothing of our conversation, if there was one. I only remember that she tried to talk to me at a school dance a few weeks later, and I gave a pinched smile and a one-word answer and turned away. There was a time and a place for niceness, and a school dance where I was already in the middle-at-best of the social hierarchy, was not that place.

My generation grew up with the catchphrase "practice random acts of kindness and senseless acts of beauty." I never figured out the "senseless beauty" bit, but I liked random acts of kindness — buying a hot dog for a guy on the street, making eye contact while giving money to a war vet on the side of the road, offering a sympathetic smile to a mom trying to juggle three children in the aisles of CVS.

One summer in college, I worked in Manhattan. On my lunch break one day, I saw a woman on the street asking for change and I invited her out to lunch. She didn't want to sit down, but we chatted the whole way through the line at a local deli. She was tall and lanky, with skin the color of almonds. She had AIDS and a cheerful countenance. I bought her a sandwich and some chips, and she clapped her hands together with one loud exclamation point when I offered a drink to go with her meal. And I never saw her again.

I hope all those moments contributed to making people's days a little brighter, but they took nothing out of me. If anything, they just made me feel good about myself. Back then, I thought kindness was about taking initiative, about offering something I had to someone in need, about being a good person. I never stopped to wonder about the sense of superiority it gave me. I never considered my own neediness. And I never thought about the source of true kindness—the kindness God has shown to me.

After all, God's kindness looked so different. It was soft-spoken. Gentle and persistent. Humble.

I remember the time I was home for Thanksgiving break during college. I was depressed and lonely and scared to go back to school. I was a mess that year—lying to people about my eating disorder, pretending to be full of piety when really I wanted nothing to do with God, relentlessly pursuing good grades at the expense of everything else in my life. Then on a cold night at my parents' house, I finally acknowledged my neediness. I said to my mother, "I just want someone to come back to school with me and hold my hand." When I finally wept, and she had nothing to offer beyond a compassionate and helpless look, I went upstairs to bed.

I pulled a dusty little prayer book off the bottom shelf of my bed stand. It was divided into categories, with Bible verses for each topic. I hadn't prayed in months. But I turned those pages to the section called "Fear," and the verse at the top of the page read, "I am the LORD, your God, who takes hold of your right hand and says to you, Do not fear; I will help you."

God was so kind to me. Not only to take hold of my hand when I had been running away, but to echo my own words so I would know he had heard me. Then, when I returned to school, having told no one of this experience, in my mailbox came a card from my grandmother with a verse printed on the inside: "I am the LORD, your God, who takes hold of your right hand and says to you, Do not fear; I will help you." My grandmother didn't send cards often and she had never sent me a card with a Bible verse on the inside. God was so kind to me.

My niceness to people — that girl in the lunchroom in middle school, the lady on the street in New York — had been motivated by some mixture of pity and curiosity and a desire to be good. God's kindness to me was motivated by love.

It wasn't until I wanted to teach my children how to be kind that I realized kindness can't really be taught. Only then did I notice that in the Bible kindness is listed as a fruit of the Spirit. It's not something we can will or create; it's something that emerges from an organic relationship with God in which God is dwelling within us and transforming our faults and failings and making us into ones who more fully act and think like his children.

Perhaps I can give my kids a foundation for kindness by teaching them to follow some basic rules — share; don't grab; use your words. Perhaps I can build on that foundation by explaining how God has been kind to me and to them, in loving us when we are unlovable, again and again. Perhaps then we will all begin to respond to the gentle nudges of the Spirit. Perhaps then we will become kind, not in random ways, but in a sustained way.

Looking back on it, kindness would have been seeing the girl alone in the lunchroom and risking my own social capital to sit down beside her — day after day after day. And now, it might mean not just offering to help my elderly neighbor get the mail, but also taking time to listen to his stories. Not because those are just "nice" things to do, but because a desire to do them overflows from the kindness God is growing in me. Because God has helped me understand that I am the recipient of such kindness — over and over and over again.

* * *

So I give up on thinking I can teach my children to be kind, though I still insist on good manners and nice deeds. And then at church one Sunday, our pastor asks adults in the congregation to choose kids to become "prayer buddies." She gives each child a form to fill out, with spaces for their names and birthdays and dreams for the future. The form includes a place to indicate whether you believe/don't believe/don't know if you believe in Jesus, as well as providing a spot for listing a prayer request.

With Penny, there are no surprises. She wants to be a teacher or a nurse when she grows up. She believes in Jesus. She wants prayer for help controlling her hands in school.

I then sit down with the form with William. He, too, offers answers I expect: "I want to be a builder." "I do believe in Jesus." But when I ask him if there is anything he wants his buddies to pray for, he says, "For help being kind."

I can only wonder why I hadn't prayed that for him, for Penny and Marilee, for myself, all along.

forgiveness

The usual notion of what Jesus did on the cross was something like this: people were so bad and so mean and God was so angry with them that he could not forgive them unless somebody big enough took the rap for the whole lot of them. Nothing could be further from the truth. Love, not anger, brought Jesus to the cross. Golgotha came as a result of God's great desire to forgive, not his reluctance.

—RICHARD J. FOSTER, *CELEBRATION OF DISCIPLINE*

Penny and William are doing everything they can to avoid getting dressed. At first, I think it's cute. She tickles him. He flaps his arms and wobbles his legs in what appears to be an imitation of a marionette dancing. They bounce on the bed. They laugh. But I am tired and Peter is out of town and the clock is ticking on a school morning.

"Guys, I really need you to get your clothes on."

I receive giggles in response.

"I'm serious. I need you both to get yourselves dressed."

Penny picks up on my tone of voice, and her face comes to attention. She sits down and starts to pull on her leggings.

But William either doesn't get it or decides to ignore me. He stands on the end of his bed and freefalls backward onto the mattress.

"William," I say, in as stern a voice as I can muster.

He stands up and returns to the footboard of the bed.

"William. If you fall onto that bed again, I will be very angry."

His eyes dart toward mine and he falls backward. His laughter sounds forced.

I grasp his arm firmly and pull him to the floor. "It is time to get dressed," I say. My jaw is tight, my nostrils flared.

He yanks his arm away, and as I move to help Penny with her socks, William climbs back onto the bed.

The constriction in my chest should be a warning that I need to walk out of the room. But I haven't learned this lesson yet. Instead, after William flops back onto the mattress for a third time, I throw his pants and shirt and sweater and underwear and I yell, "Get your pants on! Are you a baby? Are you incapable of listening to me and doing what I ask?"

He looks up at me with a scowl. He throws the clothes off the bed.

I say, "Do we really need to have a fight right now?"

He throws his pillows.

I throw them back, my eyes cold and hard. One pillow hits him in the head, not enough to hurt but enough to startle.

It breaks him. The tears burst out of his eyes and sobs erupt from his body and he says, "I just want you to help me."

I crumple. All that angry energy dissolves into remorse, and I sit next to him and hold him tight. A long time later, he gets dressed.

Once he has his clothes on, I pull him close to me again. I

trace my way through my love for him. I think about how every morning he slips his warm hand into mine as we walk down the hallway of his school. How he scrambles to my room to help me pick out my "fancy clothes" whenever I'm headed out to dinner with his dad. How he puckers up his lips for a kiss good night, good morning, and good-bye. Over my desk hangs my very favorite of his four-year-old drawings—three green peaks with a red flower and the words, "A little flower sat on a mountain. It was nighttime. The flower shivered."

He delights me. And we fight. Far too often.

I say, "William, I'm sorry I got so angry and yelled at you. Will you forgive me?"

His head is angled to the side, leaning against my shoulder. He says, "What forgive mean?"

I kiss the top of his hair. "It means it's okay between us."

He nods. "I forgive you, Momma."

We drop Penny at the bus stop and we get William and Marilee to preschool and everyone is happy, but I feel unsettled. The fight itself upset me, but my explanation of forgiveness troubles me too. I don't want William to think I am asking him to approve of my actions. They were wrong, and I can't change them now. I don't want to ask him to say it's okay that his mom yells at him and threatens him and throws pillows at him. It's not okay at all.

* * *

Forgiveness runs like a current through the Bible. It carries the story along. It meanders into the crevices and every so often pools around rocks and keeps us in one place until the current returns and we are moving again. We humans always seem to need forgiveness, from one another, from God, even from ourselves. God seems eager, always, to hand it out. Forgiveness provides the mechanism for a relationship with God here on earth and after our death. Forgiving one another is the way we are meant to demonstrate God's continued presence. And yet I forget how much I personally need God's forgiveness. I puzzle through trying to understand how Jesus' death on the cross actually affects that forgiveness. Then, even when I experience petty betrayals and hurts, I struggle to put into action the forgiveness I've experienced.

I believe in forgiveness. And it confounds me.

I return often to one particular Bible scene about forgiveness. It's an odd story. Jesus is speaking to a crowd of religious teachers inside a house. All of a sudden, a paralyzed man is lowered in front of Jesus through a hole in the roof. The man's friends, desperate to get him to Jesus, interrupt the lesson, vandalize the house, and put on public display this man who cannot walk.

But what seems most peculiar to me about this story is Jesus' response. He has been healing people left and right, so I think it's reasonable to assume this man is looking for the same physical healing others have received. But Jesus looks at him and says, "Son, your sins are forgiven."

His statement prompts outrage among the religion scholars in attendance because Jesus isn't supposed to offer forgiveness — that's God's job. But what did it prompt in the paralyzed man? Did he lay there thinking, "Um, Jesus, that's really nice and everything, but what about my legs?"

Jesus goes on to heal the man of his paralysis too, but the forgiveness comes first. The physical healing seems almost to be an afterthought.

It makes me wonder whether Jesus is trying to communicate something about what forgiveness does to our souls. I wonder whether he's trying to help us understand that forgiveness is more important than physical prowess. That forgiveness is itself healing. That forgiveness enables us to walk again.

I think of the time I came home with all three kids from our weekly Music Together class. Penny and William had bickered already during the car ride. It was six o'clock, and Peter was still coaching at a tennis match, so I scrambled to get dinner together on my own. Penny dumped a box of unused Valentines onto the table. "Penny," I said sharply, "control your hands. And William, turn your place mat to the flower side so I can put your plate on it."

I returned to the kitchen and came back with their dinners. Penny was prone across the table, reaching for an orange Tinkertoy. William was slapping the place mat against the wood, cork side up. In a matter of seconds, I pulled Penny into her seat and threw the place mat across the room. Just as quickly, William was sobbing. Penny's remorseful little face peered up at me, her eyes pooling with tears even as she bit her lip. Marilee, not quite clear on the source of the problem, nevertheless had taken to mimicking her brother and sister, so she started yelling.

It took a few minutes to calm everyone down. I was close to tears and sick of myself and the constant repetitive squabbles. I remembered the instructions William's preschool teacher offered for kids who struggled to control their emotions—deep breaths and big hugs. And, after a few minutes, I remembered that we could pray. So we prayed for God's presence to come into our household. We prayed for peace amidst the chaos and for love amidst the anger. We let the food go cold and we sat down together and shared how we each had made a bad choice.

"I made a bad choice when I didn't listen, Mom," said William. I nodded approvingly.

Then he said, "And you made a bad choice when you threw my place mat across the room."

I stifled a giggle and nodded again. Then we all said, "I'm sorry." And we all said, "I forgive you."

The pattern continues today: Children disobey. Mother erupts. Everyone cries. Everyone says, "I forgive you." But William's question to me so recently — "What forgive mean?" — helps me realize that my children have been obediently parroting my words without understanding their intent. Our practice of forgiveness has built a scaffold, a guide for what they are supposed to say after an argument. But so far this structure has been built without walls or floors. For us to stand on it, we have more work to do.

* * *

A few days after the pillow-throwing incident and my insufficient explanation of forgiveness, William and I are reading a book in which a father comes home from work late and asks his wife to forgive him. William pauses and asks again, "What forgive mean?"

This time I'm ready. I say, "It means that even though someone has done something wrong, you won't stay mad at them and you won't try to make them feel bad about doing something wrong. It means you will be friends with them again, even though they hurt you. Just like God forgives us and loves us even though we do wrong things."

He nods and takes my hand in his.

Over the years I have heard many stories of dramatic forgiveness: the priest in *Les Mis* who forgives Jean Valjean for stealing his silver, a magazine article about parents who forgive their daughter's murderer, a book about a marriage restored when the husband forgives his wife's adultery. But the stories of forgiveness in my own life are far more mundane. Forgiving Peter when he comes home late from work without letting me know. Needing his forgiveness when I gossip about his colleague and share information that should have remained confidential. Forgiving myself after I snap at the kids yet another time. Forgiving them when they look at me with meanness behind their eyes.

My kids don't fully understand the meaning of the word *forgive*. They have helped me realize that I don't fully understand it either. But together, I hope we are learning how to live out what forgiveness looks like in daily life. Even though we continue to wound each other, I hope we will also continue to invite Jesus' healing presence into our midst. That we will all experience the life-giving power that enables us to walk again.

Forgiveness is as domestic as it is dramatic. And for all the drama of the cross, the language of the Bible is that of a domestic story of a Father forgiving his children, entreating them to return home.

church

It is madness to wear ladies' straw hats and velvet hats
to church; we should all be wearing crash helmets.
Ushers should issue life preservers and signal flares;
they should lash us to our pews. For the sleeping god
may wake someday and take offense, or the waking
god may draw us out to where we can never return.

—ANNIE DILLARD, *TEACHING A STONE TO TALK*

Our kids wake up a good four hours before the service starts.
Peter and I allow each child to choose something to watch on
TV. I sleep for another hour, until 7:30. Peter goes for a run. We
eat bagels. Somehow we still scramble to get everyone clean
and dressed and out the door. Then each child has a different
strong opinion about which parent should drive. Finally, I take
the wheel, and five minutes later we arrive at church, late.

Marilee heads downstairs to the nursery with Peter, and I
sneak in the side door with the older two. Our entrance becomes
more conspicuous as William tugs my hand all the way up the
aisle to our typical spot in the first pew.

Ours is a small congregation of fifty people or so most Sundays. We chose this church because it was close to our home,

and the preaching was good, and the pastor had young children like us, and, unlike the bigger churches twenty minutes away, this one allowed us to stay connected to our local community. A few other families with young children attend, but the average age hovers around sixty-five. I am starting to remember the names of the faithful folks who show up every week—Ginnie, Margaret, Rod, Jack, Suzy. They smile at us as we file past.

A few minutes after we claim our pew, Penny lies down on her stomach, chin propped on her hands. I tug her back into a seated position. William watches attentively until the choir sits down from its introit. Now he takes his children's program and places it on top of a hymnal. He bears down with a pencil and scribbles across the picture of Jesus feeding the five thousand with large bold gray strokes, as if he is trying to bury the image under a torrent of lead. I try to make my whisper both very quiet and very forceful as I lean toward his ear: "Could you please color gently?"

It is time for the prayer of confession. I bow my head but keep my eyes open, attuned to the possibility of disruption on either side. Penny opens the hymnal and starts to sing. I put my hand over her mouth. Irritation feels like it has weight, like it is tracing a line up my spine that will soon extend to my shoulders and seep down my arms. Peter is still downstairs, which either means that Marilee is inconsolable about his absence, or, more likely, that the child care person hasn't shown up.

Soon someone is in the pulpit. She reads something from the Bible about God's love for us and how we should love one another. But I am shushing my children and can't pay attention to the words I am hearing.

I am tired. William is still scribbling. Penny glares in my

direction every time I close the hymnal on her lap. I stretch my neck and finally give way to the thought I have held at bay for months: I want to give up on church as a family.

* * *

I grew up going to church every week. I remember my own mother tugging my arm when I wanted to lie down on the soft red cushioned pew. I remember the kneeling and the collection plate and scampering down the aisle with the other kids when it was finally time to head out for Sunday school.

I never questioned the fact of our attendance, even when we moved from an Episcopal church in North Carolina to a Presbyterian one in Connecticut, even as I grew older and other kids negotiated with their parents for another day to sleep in. I showed up. I sang in the choir. I sat through confirmation class. I smiled at the adults. I tried to listen to the sermons.

But my most powerful experience of God didn't come in the midst of a worship service on a Sunday morning; it came over the summer of my sophomore year in high school when I was at a Christian camp. This moment of communion solidified my faith, but it didn't convince me that church was particularly helpful or even important in the life of a Christian. I became a less frequent church attender as my "personal" relationship with God began to grow.

In college, I decided to investigate. I spent a few Sunday mornings with an African-American congregation. I loved the music, but the three-hour service was too much for me. I tried an Episcopal church once. The minister used a purple dinosaur named Figment as her main sermon illustration. I never went back. I tried conservative churches and liberal ones. The spoken prayers, the music, and the sermon were my points of reference, my reasons for critique or commendation. I liked the grandeur of the Episcopal liturgy and the intimacy of the Assemblies of God worship time. I liked the simplicity of the Presbyterians and the warmth of the Baptists. But I never stayed long enough to get to know anyone or to let anyone get to know me.

* * *

That afternoon, once Marilee has woken up from her nap, we drive out to the lake. It is still early spring, so we are alone as a family by the water. All three kids spend an hour filling cups and pouring them in the sand and digging and forming sand castles and stomping on them. Back and forth and up and down, building, smoothing, discovering. Peter and I watch with a sense of wonder. Marilee, growing more into herself every day, navigating three steps without holding on to the railing. William, always inquisitive, crouching low at the water's edge to watch as it laps against the shore. Penny, ever the big sister, helping Marilee build.

I start to consider whether this time on the beach is the spiritual one, the one with beauty and goodness and laughter emerging naturally, without any effort other than a stack of plastic cups for entertainment. Again comes the thought: *I wonder if we ought to abandon church altogether.* I mentally list the reasons we might as well stay home. We are a nuisance to the others with our loud scribbles and always-moving bodies. We are irritated with the erratic child care and the only occasional Sunday school teachers. We could sing our own songs and read our own Scripture and say our own prayers and not even bother to get out of our pajamas. Then we could go outside and praise God along with the created order.

But just as powerful in my memory as the disruptions we caused this morning is the recollection of Easter Sunday a few weeks back. Easter had come as a surprise this year. I hadn't tried to give anything up for Lent. My only intention for those forty days had been to pray, using a prayer book, once in the morning and once at night. I hadn't even kept up that practice, nor had I done anything to get the kids thinking about the upcoming holy day. Instead, those weeks included my own grumbling and a bad fight with Peter and harsh words for the children.

I was as distracted as ever that Easter day. Marilee was crying in the nursery, and Peter and I took turns comforting her. William wanted to kneel on the floor to provide a better setup for his coloring. Penny wanted to read out loud from the Bible during the prayer time. But still, I gazed at the white cloth draped over the cross and took in the sight of white lilies in full exuberant bloom and I sang, "Christ the Lord is risen today, Alleluia!"

My faithlessness had changed nothing, and I could hardly believe it. It almost shocked me to realize the tomb was empty regardless of my acknowledgment of that new and world-changing reality. It felt like an affront to my sense of significance to see I was still invited to the celebration, as distracted and self-consumed as I had been. God was still God, regardless of my squirming children and my scattered thoughts and my very ordinary and prayerless days. And church was the place where I remembered that steadiness, that faithfulness, that constancy. Church was the place where if I lost my faith, God's faithfulness would be found, waiting for me.

I shake myself out of my reverie as the kids finally show

signs of hunger. We rinse the sand from our feet and pack up the towels and cups. On our drive home as we pass the church building again, William yells, "Look! It's our church!"

All three kids erupt in delighted laughter.

It is a place that holds joy for them, somehow. Joy and, I suspect, comfort. It is a place where they are known, a little bit, by everyone from the youngest children to the oldest grandmothers. It is a place where everyone assumes that God is present and deserves to be worshiped. It is a place where prayer and Scripture and singing hymns are expected. But it is also a place that requires something of them — sitting still, paying attention, subjecting their desires to those of the community. It is a place that gives to them but also asks of them. A place that gives to and asks of me also.

It wasn't until I was in my early thirties that I learned that whenever Paul writes the word *you* in Scripture, it is plural. I had always read most of Paul's instructions as individual ones, written to me, singular. But our Bibles could read "y'all" almost every time Paul offers a command, a rebuke, or a word of encouragement. Paul can't conceive of an individual Christian divorced from the church. Christianity happens in community as we bear one another's burdens — whether the burden of calming our wriggly kids or using a cane to walk through the front door or asking for prayer for a neighbor's son who broke his leg in a car crash yesterday.

Church is not a guarantee. I assume my children will grow up with doubts. They may very well walk away from this faith we are trying to pass along. My goal is not to dictate what they believe or to think that if only we do this right they will live for the rest of their days as Christians. But I do want to lay out a net for them. I want to introduce them to a place where the old and young, rich and poor, those from different races and backgrounds, will welcome them as they are. When they encounter suffering or betrayal or heartache, I want them to have a safe place to fall. When they find themselves in need or in pain, when their lives are coming apart, I pray they will land in the arms of a God who has and does and will love them. And I believe church may be just that place, whether it is a cathedral with lofty liturgy and thousands of worshipers or a little country sanctuary with a few grandparents nodding in the pews.

So we will go back, next week and the week after that and the week after that. We will trust — even amidst my short-tempered words and their inability to sit still and their refusal to go up front for the children's message — we will trust they are learning something about what it means to be a part of the body of Christ, something about God's presence in the midst of a very ordinary place in a very ordinary town, something about God's grace and love, something about singing Alleluia, praise the Lord.

money

How many times have I been put at the front of the line without even knowing there was a line? How many times have I walked through a door that opened, invisibly and silently, for me, but slammed shut for others? How many lines have I cut in a life of privilege?

—ANDY CROUCH, *PLAYING GOD*

We sit on the porch of our house near the Connecticut shore at six o'clock in the evening. The sun bathes half the table in light. We are five days into our vacation as a family, and I am thinking about the gifts gathered in this place, as if the faces of my children and the smell of the marsh and the sound of the waves lapping against the rocky coastline have been piled up in front of me and can be opened one by one.

I think about Marilee's sweetness—her pronouncement earlier that day as I carried her downstairs after her nap: "Mommy, I like you and I love you. You make me feel very happy." I think about the way I laughed and laughed this morning when Penny said, "Mom, I have two funny stories. One, I got run over by a car and I only scraped my knee. Two, I got run over by a doctor and I only banged my elbow!" And I think about William's

196

constant observations, like at lunchtime today when he said, "Mom, I think this floor is aquamarine. Or teal. Or maybe a color in between aquamarine and teal."

Marilee begins our meal the way she usually does. "Say a bwessing?" she asks.

We hold hands and she sings, "Tank you, Fader," to the tune of "Frère Jacques." We respond in kind as she leads us: "For dis food. And our many bwessings. Ah-ah-men."

The kids are quiet as they dig in to their pasta and hot dogs and carrots.

Peter puts his hands behind his head and leans back in his chair. "Guys, do you know that we have been given so much?"

Penny and William glance at each other as if they need some guidance on how to respond.

"I mean, this house alone," Peter says, hands sweeping outward to take in the lawn and the porch and the shoreline in the distance. "It is such a gift. Such a blessing."

I assume he's thinking about his mom, whose untimely death provided an inheritance to make a down payment on the house. And about my family, whose century-long residence on this little strip of coastline has helped this place become home for us. And about the undeserved beauty and spaciousness and peace it all brings.

"Dad," William asks, "how much does this house cost? A thousand dollars?"

Peter holds back a smile as he says, "More than that, William."

"A bajillion dollars?"

"Well, not quite that much. But still, a lot of money. We have been given a lot of money, and we get to use it for the things we need, like clothes and books and food, but we also get to use it for all sorts of really exciting things, like this house and sometimes giving it away to other people who don't have what we have."

William's forehead wrinkles. He stabs a piece of his hot dog and says, "I don't want to give my money away. I only want to save it for things I want to buy." His face contorts, nose scrunched, lips pursed.

William has been fascinated with money for about a year. I think it started when he received twenty dollars for his fourth birthday, which prompted a trip to the toy store. He selected his own gift: Emily, from the Thomas the Train series. He has been on a quest for more money ever since. He routinely scours the car for stray coins. He sometimes plays "look for money" if we can't come up with another activity. Once he woke up from a nap inconsolable. He finally calmed down enough to gasp, "Mom, I just need a piece of money." After he held a quarter in his hand, all was well.

Peter says, "That's fine. But one day maybe you will want to give some money away."

William's face isn't quite as dour as it had been a moment earlier, but he is still squinting, as if he doesn't trust his father's words.

I say, "Actually, in the Bible, God and Jesus ask us to give some of our money away."

He shakes his head at me. The scowl returns.

"I don't mean give it all away." I start talking more quickly. "So, you might have ten dollars and decide to give one dollar away to help other people."

"Or to the church," Peter says.

"Or even two dollars," I add. "If you had a hundred then you might want to give away ten or twenty. And you would still have eighty left for yourself."

"Well," William says, his head tilted a little to one side, "maybe." He returns to his pasta.

* * *

When I was a kid I would count the days until Sunday, when we received our allowances. I was required to place one dime in the collection plate at church each week, but the other ninety cents were mine to hold. My mother accompanied me to the bank when I was seven years old and I possessed six dollars, enough to begin my first savings account. I cherished the ledger that kept track of deposits and withdrawals. A few years later, it thrilled me to calculate the effect compounding interest might have on my investments, as long as I didn't spend anything. I remember what I think William feels — that desire for more money, the pleasure of counting it and putting it in order and imagining what it might buy.

One night when I was seven or eight, I grew frustrated with how slowly my money collection was growing. My piggy bank at that moment was a tall red plastic cat. It had a slit at the top, but the only way to extract the coins was to cut the bank open. Mom had told me I would need to wait to open it until I had filled it all the way up. I had about eight inches of coins to go.

So that night, I snuck up to my father's office on the third floor of our house. He kept his spare change in piles on his desk, sorted according to type. I plucked four quarters from the top of one pile, scampered back to my bedroom, and dropped them into my bank. I felt no satisfaction. The coins didn't make a dent in the cavern that remained between my meager collection of dimes and pennies and the goal of a full bank. Worse, I started to wonder whether Dad knew how much money was in those piles on his desk. It suddenly felt as though someone had struck me behind my windpipe. I turned the cat upside down, frantic to retrieve and return the coins. But I was stuck.

The next evening, I asked my mother, "Do you think I could have my allowance early?"

"You have to wait until Sunday, sweetie. You know that. Why?"

The story tumbled out. "I just want my allowance so I can pay Dad back." I didn't want to admit my wrongdoing without being able to make it right at the same time. But Mom said no.

My dad was sitting in a reclining armchair in the den. I climbed into his lap and began to cry. I told him everything, and he patted me on the back and forgave me my debt. He didn't even want my allowance when it came that Sunday.

I look back on that moment as my first experience of grace, though I'm not sure in retrospect how much it changed me. I still dreamed of being wealthy when I got older. I still insisted on being the banker in games of Monopoly. And I still saw any money I received as belonging entirely to me.

* * *

The next morning, William walks in circles around the kitchen with a long blue plastic tube as his prop. He tries to balance it on his nose and it crashes to the floor. As he stoops down to pick it up, I say, "Buddy, I'm thinking about our conversation last night about giving money away."

His eyes narrow just a bit. He picks up the tube.

"I wish I had talked about it a little differently," I say. "I told you we should give a little bit of our money away because God tells us to, but what I should have said is that everything we have belongs to God."

He says, "Mom, have you ever tooken a stick like this and made it spin without falling down?"

"Taken," I say. "No. And that stick doesn't belong inside. But, William, about the money ..."

He is intent on the stick. It clatters to the floor again and I shoo him onto the porch.

I start to clear the breakfast dishes, and once again I want to take back my words from the night before. My instinct was to offer a set of rules and percentages, a checklist to ensure obedient generosity. I had wanted to reassure him that giving didn't need to be radical or sacrificial. But I wonder whether my instincts betray my heart. I wonder whether I really believe what I wish I had explained—that everything we have has been given to us by God. That we have the privilege of using it for good—for us and for others. That we have been blessed in order to be a blessing.

As I rinse Eggo waffle crumbs into the sink and load the dishwasher with bowls and cups and utensils, I think back to a conversation with our friend Paul Miller about the effect of money. He explained that money usually leads to greater individualism—separate bedrooms for each child, separate cars, houses far apart from one another, individual televisions and phones and devices. But he pointed out that money can also serve as a means of bringing people together, of celebrating relationships and beauty and the abundant goodness of this life. Using money wisely requires a relationship with God, not a set of rules. Rather than a checklist, it depends on a prayerful conversation about spending and saving and giving, about generosity and sacrifice and hospitality and pleasure.

I think about telling William the story of the rich young ruler who walked away from Jesus sad. I could wield it to try to convince my son that generosity is the better course. Or I could help him to justify his desires by calling on the story of Levi, the tax collector who "leaves everything" to follow Jesus and then proceeds to have a party at his house. (Apparently "leaving everything" still permitted him to provide wine and food and a place in which to enjoy it.)

Or I could try to show him what it looks like to trust God with all that we have. I could try to live a life of radical generosity in response to God's graciousness to us. I could try to take great delight in the material provision of our lives, even as I hold our things loosely and offer them readily for the use and blessing of others. I could save money for the good of our family and not because I fear the future. I could enter into a conversation with God and others about how to use the gifts we have been given. I could let go of rules and invite William into an ongoing conversation not only about allowances and collection plates but also about the needs of the world and the ways we can respond.

William comes back inside as I get the dishwasher going.

"Let's get ready to go to the beach," I say.

I hold out my hand and he takes it and we walk up the stairs together.

We have been given so much.

friendship

"Why did you do all this for me?" he asked. "I don't deserve it. I've never done anything for you."

"You have been my friend," replied Charlotte. "That in itself is a tremendous thing."

—E. B. WHITE, *CHARLOTTE'S WEB*

The first playdate does not go well. Emma comes over after school with Penny. They walk hand in hand from the bus stop to our back door, and I try not to hover as Penny shows Emma inside. Emma, with her big eyes and silvery blonde hair, is as new to town as we are. Penny has been asking to have her over for two months.

At first they are content with their apple slices and corn chips. But soon Emma seems fidgety—impatient, I imagine, with Penny's slow eating. As they clear their dishes, I whisper to Penny, "Why don't you ask Emma what she wants to do?"

Penny turns to her friend, "What do you want to do?"

"Dance party?" Emma asks.

Penny wrinkles her forehead.

I turn on some Louis Armstrong, our family's favorite dance

music. Now it is Emma's turn to look confused. "Do you have Taylor Swift?" she asks.

I quickly create a Taylor Swift station on Pandora, but soon Emma is standing alone in the middle of the pop-music-filled family room. Penny has retreated to the couch, where she sits reading a Magic Tree House book out loud.

"Do you want to play dress up?" Emma asks.

Penny shakes her head. I stand in the doorway, trying to decide if I should explain to Emma that it's hard for Penny to take clothes on and off, that she has never loved imaginative play.

Penny says, "How about a board game?"

Emma's enthusiasm for the whole afternoon seems to have waned. She shakes her head. "I don't like any board games. At all."

Emma ends up finding a willing participant for both dress up and a dance party in William. Penny stays on the couch until Emma goes home.

And I feel as though I am stuck in that doorway, always in between knowing whether I should intervene or let these relationships run their course, wanting to allow Penny to advocate for herself but remembering the mother of an older child with Down syndrome who warned me that I would need to do a lot of shepherding to help her form friendships. It has been like this for years, and I have never figured out the balance. The knot at the back of my throat has become familiar, alongside the question I don't want to ask again: Will it ever be easy for Penny to make friends?

* * *

I take some comfort that Penny and William have been friends with each other for years. I remember their first day of preschool together, when they got ready with new backpacks—Dora for Penny and Spiderman for her brother. They wore back-to-school outfits that included a green and pink dress for Penny and a bright orange shirt with jeans for William. We took the requisite photos, buckled the kids into their car seats, and headed out.

William entered the two-year-old room and Penny joined the other four-year-olds. But I picked William up at school without his big sister. She spent her afternoons at the local integrated preschool program, and the bus dropped her off at our house at four o'clock.

Once William realized this pattern was permanent, he scowled and said, "Why Penny still at school? Why she not at home with me?"

One afternoon during her absence, he and I watched *Bambi* together. Near the end, when spring arrived, all the little animals fell in love. The owl called them "twitterpated." William said, "What twitterpated mean?"

"Well," I said, "it's kind of like they become super-great friends. Like your dad and I are super-great friends."

His tipped his head back and looked at the ceiling, as if he needed to focus on a blank space in order to process my words. But then he nodded, and a smile spread across his face. "Oh. Like Penny and I are super-great friends."

I squeezed his leg. "Yes. Kind of like that."

During that first year of preschool, Penny got off her little bus and I asked her about her day. "Good," she said. She then sat on the bench by our kitchen table, happily munching on crackers. Her face was almost as round as it had been when she was a baby, and her eyes sparkled. She offered no clue of discontent. But I often uncovered a note in her backpack that read something like, "Penny had a hard day today. She knocked over her friends' blocks and tugged at their clothes repeatedly, even after redirection and realizing some of the consequences of her behavior. Do you have any suggestions for how we can better handle this in the future?"

I didn't know how to handle it better. My best guess was that Penny wanted to befriend those other kids. But I didn't know how to teach her to do it. I could try to explain that she might tug clothes or pull hair or even pinch a classmate as a way, in her mind, to initiate a friendship. I could talk about her impulsivity and how we were working on it. But all my explanations wouldn't help the other kids understand. It might not even help the teachers.

Sometimes I wondered if we would be the only ones who knew her like this—as an easygoing, funny, helpful kid with a big heart. I wondered if—I feared that—we would be the only ones who got to call her our friend.

* * *

When Penny was first born, fear buried me for months. In the initial days after her delivery, I was afraid she would die young. I was afraid she would never talk. I was afraid she would never get married. I was afraid I would stop loving her. I was afraid I wouldn't think she was beautiful. And I was afraid she would never make friends.

I was able to climb out of most of those fears with time and information. I learned that the life expectancy of children with Down syndrome has increased dramatically. I realized that my love for her only grew, and that it had nothing to do with her chromosome count. I began to believe that just as we could communicate with each other through nursing and cuddling, we would be able to communicate with each other throughout her life, regardless of her ability to speak. I let go of my fears about marriage and beauty and school and the future and focused on loving her right now. Except with friendship. I was still afraid she would never make friends.

As the years went on, that fear often pushed me back into my own sense of inadequacy. I felt guilty that I didn't arrange more playdates. But having a child and her mother over to our house felt like an inconvenient interruption within an already busy schedule. Also, I didn't know many of the other moms whose kids went to Penny's school. And I've never been good at coming up with projects for kids to do together. Beyond that, I told myself, Penny was usually exhausted by the end of her school day. On the rare occasion we had someone over, Penny often ended up reading a book by herself or snuggling in the other kid's mom's lap.

So my fear remained, in part because I knew I could be doing more to help Penny develop friendships and in part because I knew that friendships really matter.

* * *

On the night before Jesus died, he told his disciples he no longer called them servants; instead, he called them friends. I understand servitude. Jesus is in charge. I'm supposed to show up and take orders and hurry out to obey. But being a friend is less well-defined. It means I show up and sit down for a cup of tea and listen and talk, and we laugh and cry and work together.

It means reciprocity. It means breaking bread. It means choosing someone to whom no generational tie exists and being with them, faithfully, lovingly, forever.

It means that friendship is a gift from God. It means friendship is important. It means I should continue to hope for friendship for Penny.

Years ago, I wrote down on a prayer card my request that God would help Penny make friends. I added more specific requests along the way. That she and William would become friends. That other people would invite her over for playdates. That she would make one good friend at school. Some days I just peered at that card with longing. I underlined the word *friends*, twice. Then I circled it, as if I needed to make sure God knew I really meant it.

Then, at ballet class, back when Penny was in preschool, one of the moms wrote her name and phone number on a napkin. "Why don't you call us so we can have Penny over for a playdate? My daughter would just love that."

The playdate went fine, and we had the mom and daughter over to our house the next time. But kindergarten rolled around, and that family wasn't in the same school. We didn't go to that ballet studio anymore, and when we passed them in the grocery store, we said hi but we didn't talk about a time to get together.

But a month into kindergarten, Penny asked if we could invite her friend Anna over after school. When I picked them up, Anna was jumping up and down. We started walking, and I couldn't suppress my smile at these little girls with their oversized backpacks ahead of me. Soon they were talking and I was in the background, trying to listen in without interrupting their conversation. Then Anna reached out and took Penny's hand. As if they were, well, friends.

Anna came to our house a second time. They held hands again. When we got home and ate a snack, I asked, "What was the best thing about school today?"

Penny said, "Playing with Anna."

Anna said, "Playing with Penny, until she ran into a pole on the playground and had to go to the nurse."

Penny proudly displayed the bump on her head: "I was brave. I didn't cry. I got ice."

For Penny's sixth birthday, she opted for a day with Anna instead of a party with multiple kids. I took them out for pizza. They chose a booth designed for one person and snuggled next to each other. They held hands and giggled, and Penny said, "Anna! You are so FUNNY!" and then later, "I have some super-exciting news announcement. I have a puppy named Sparky."

Penny beamed, and Anna giggled again.

But a few months later came our move. I knew Penny's behavior tended to be rough on other kids at the start of a new school year. I knew moving and Peter's new job would be stressful and distracting and I wouldn't facilitate play very well. It felt as though the answer to prayer we found in Anna had been revoked. When I thought about Penny and Anna, my throat felt thick, as though I was trying hard to swallow but the food had gotten stuck. Those prayer cards with years of notes to God about Penny and friendship were lost in the move and I didn't re-create them. During our first year in town, we invited a few kids from Penny's class over, but, like Emma, they mostly played with William.

* * *

Still, throughout the spring, we start to see Emma more and more. Her parents work at the same school as Peter, so we bump into each other at sporting events and all-school picnics. One day, Penny and Emma and I are walking through campus. Emma's mom has agreed that she can come home with us until the lacrosse game is over. As we walk, Penny throws her arms out wide. "Emma is my BFF!" she exclaims as they embrace.

Emma looks pensive. "Penny, you are definitely one of my BFF's," she says. Then she looks at me. "Sometimes Penny asks the same question over and over again."

Penny shrugs, as if she can offer no explanation.

I say, "Well, sometimes Penny does that when she's excited. Right, Pen? One of the things I do at home is remind her that she can make a statement—like, instead of asking over and over again if you're going to have a playdate today, she could say, 'I'm so excited you're coming over!'"

Penny stops walking and looks at Emma. "I'm so excited you're coming over!"

We get home, and Penny and Emma share a snack. They start to play with Play-Doh. I wash dishes and put away plates and clear Penny's backpack of the day's forms and announcements. Their chatter turns to planning, and soon they are outside on the play set. I listen through the window—Emma is the doctor and Penny is the patient. Soon they need my help for a minute while they get married, Penny to "Fred" and Emma to "Max." To my surprise and delight, they are hugging each other.

And I begin to see that my role in helping Penny make friends is to hope. I cannot force other seven-year-olds to choose her. I cannot guarantee that Emma will still be her friend next week, much less through the harrowing social years of middle school and beyond. But in their fledgling friendship I can see the heart of a man who no longer calls us servants. I recognize the imprint of the one who has chosen me as a friend.

My prayer began as a prayer of fear. It is now a prayer of hope.

baptism

Long before we ever get around to asking questions about God, God has been questioning us ... We are known before we know.

—EUGENE PETERSON, *RUN WITH THE HORSES*

Ever the dutiful mother, I am reading email on my phone as I wander home from the post office with William and Marilee. As I scan my messages I see a note from our pastor inviting anyone in our congregation to get baptized. I wonder out loud, "William, do you want to get baptized?"

He is walking slowly. "Mom, did you know that's a sycamore tree?"

"No. I didn't." I smile and turn my full attention to my son. "How can you tell?"

"Well, Nana told me, but you can figure it out by the bark."

It is a beautiful tree, with a thick trunk and strong sprawling branches.

"Bud, do you know what it means to get baptized?"

He shakes his head, still gazing at the tree.

We used to attend a church that offered infant dedication rather than infant baptism. The practice of infant dedication taps into a centuries-old theological struggle over the significance and purpose of baptism. Some Christians believed that the Bible upheld infant baptism as a sign of God's faithfulness not only to individuals but to entire families; others believed that baptism needed to be a personal decision in response to an experience of God's grace. Peter and I were sympathetic to both arguments, but ultimately we stuck with the traditions in which we were raised. We believe in infant baptism because we believe that God is always the one who initiates relationship, always the one on whom we are dependent for grace, even when we are too young to respond.

So when Penny was eleven months old, we arranged for a special service of baptism with a pastor friend who traveled from Virginia to New Jersey for the day. Over a hundred people — family, friends, Peter's colleagues and students — were in attendance. It was a blessed day of receiving her and celebrating her as our daughter, a beloved member of the family of God.

We had intended to do the same, though perhaps with less fanfare, when William and Marilee were born. We managed to get them dedicated at our home church, but the dates for a baptism celebration never quite worked out. Our pastor friend from Virginia had kids of his own, and it was harder and harder to make our schedules line up. We were busy. Multiple moves had consumed nearly two years of energy. Soon enough William was five, and it wasn't so clear that we could make this decision on his behalf anymore.

So, as he peers through the branches of the sycamore tree, I explain, "Well, it means you decide you want God to be with you forever. You either get water dripped on your head or you can dunk your whole body in a lake as a way to show that you want God with you always."

He nods slowly. "Water dripped on my head. Not in a lake."

"So are you saying you would want that?"

He nods but doesn't say anything.

We start walking again, bumping along the uneven sidewalk.

"Why is it that way?" he asks. "Why water?"

I think about Jesus' baptism. I think about the waters at creation. The flood. The River Jordan. The Red Sea. But instead of giving a lesson in biblical imagery, I ask him, "What does water do?"

"Well," he says, stopping to pick up a stick from the ground, "it cleans dishes."

I nod with an encouraging smile. "What else? What about these trees?"

"Oh! It helps them grow."

"Is there anything else we do with water?"

"We drink it when we're thirsty."

That seems like a good enough list to me. "So, buddy, water helps us get clean and grow and feel better when we're thirsty. God is the same way. You know how sometimes we feel like we're dirty on the inside when we hurt somebody else? Well, baptism is a way of reminding us that God cleans us from our sin so we aren't dirty anymore. And just like water helps a plant grow, the Holy Spirit helps us grow into the people we want to be, who God wants us to be. And just like water makes us feel better when we're thirsty, having God in our life makes us feel better. So do you want that? Do you want to get baptized?"

Marilee, from her seat in the stroller, says, "I don' wanna get 'tized!"

William squats down and looks at her. "Marilee. It means

you would be with God forever." His voice is suddenly higher-pitched than usual, and his eyes are wide open, as earnest as he can make them.

She scowls. "I don' wanna be God fowevah!"

He shakes his head with a little laugh. "You wouldn't BE God. You would be WITH God."

She pinches her face together, as if she has made an irrevocable decision to be disagreeable, and says, in her best impression of a fifteen-year-old, "I don' wanna get 'tized!"

I relate the conversation to Peter later that night, and we set up a time to talk with our pastor. We arrive early at church the next Sunday, and she explains baptism to both William and Marilee. They nod with big eyes. Then she smiles at Peter and me and says, "Baptism is as much about you two and about the rest of us in this congregation, pledging ourselves to raise these kids to know how much God loves them."

Within a week, we have a date on the calendar and the extended family is making plans to come to town.

* * *

Peter and I were both baptized as infants. We can't remember the occasions, of course, other than by looking at the photograph of Peter in a navy blue sailor suit, laughing in the arms of his mom and dad. They flew to Denmark, his dad's homeland, for the ceremony, and a minister — someone Peter never met again — pronounced the words of welcome into the family of God. My mom probably has photos of my baptism somewhere too — the font in a little historic Episcopal church in a small town in North Carolina, a long white gown, a baby crying. I have a certificate to prove it happened.

But for years after those moments, it wouldn't have been obvious to an outside observer that God was present in any particular way in our lives. Peter was more of a troublemaker than I was—he chased girls and beat up on his little brother and lied and cheated and stole stuff, in fairly typical middle-school-boy fashion. In high school, he drank and tried pot and chased girls some more and pursued the life of a moderately rebellious boy who did things like throwing a large, wooden bench down three flights of stairs at school just to see what would happen.

I played by all the rules—no drinking or smoking. Nothing beyond flirting with boys. Plenty of moral reprehension at the tales of some of my classmates' behavior.

Both of us went to church—he when his mother insisted, I dutifully on Sunday mornings. But neither of us could have said with any conviction that we loved God. Neither of us thought about God much at all, really.

And neither of us ever had a dramatic experience of being "born again." Neither of us can pinpoint the exact moment when we "became" Christians. I had that powerful moment of prayer when God spoke to me midway through high school, but I wouldn't have called it a conversion at the time. Perhaps I was already a Christian, but at that moment God became active in my life. As if the Spirit had been waiting, since my infancy, for me to notice his presence.

Peter, similarly, wandered toward faith intermittently for the final two years of high school. He met me around the same time he became interested in whether there was a God who cared about him, a spiritual reality that might matter in his life. But it took years before it was clear he wasn't going back.

So was it baptism that made us Christians? As infants, without any will to speak of, were we born into this faith we now hold dear? Or was it a decision we made, however long it took, as adolescents and adults? Was it a matter of family or intellect or emotion or will? Or a slow recognition that God had been holding on to us all along?

* * *

The baptism Sunday arrives, and Peter's father bestows a silver cross necklace on both Marilee and William. William wears it with some degree of awe. He chooses his only pair of pants without a hole in the knee, along with a buttoned-down shirt and a striped sweater. He searches for his penny loafers. Marilee approaches her outfit with equal concern, and she ends up in a hot pink bubble dress and white leggings. "Do I look booful, Momma?" she asks. She knows exactly how I will reply.

Before the service begins, Marilee spots her Nana in the sanctuary. She runs to greet her, exuberant, and hits her head on the corner of a pew. The tears erupt and she cannot stop crying. I carry her to the foyer until she becomes calm.

But it is a long wait from the start of the service to the baptism itself, and Marilee never quite settles down. She wriggles. She wants to climb over me to see her grandparents. She wants a snack. She tries to squirm her body under the pew.

At long last, all five of us surround the baptismal font. Penny and William scamper behind the pulpit as our pastor reads the introduction. Marilee takes off in the opposite direction. I am off balance, wearing high-heeled boots instead of my customary clogs, tottering after my children in view of the whole congregation.

Then the time comes for them to be baptized. First, William answers our pastor's questions.

Do you now desire to be baptized in the name of the Father, Son, and Holy Spirit?

Do you repent of your sins, confessing Christ as your Savior and Lord and living as his faithful disciple?

Empowered by the Holy Spirit, will you do all in your power to participate fully in the life of this congregation, to do justice, to love kindness, and to walk humbly with your God?

"I do. I do. I will," he says.

She pours a handful of water over his forehead, and he receives it with his eyes closed.

Marilee's turn comes, and she recoils from my arms. I hold her as best I can as Peter and I promise to renounce the powers of evil, to teach the word of God, to pray for her. But when our pastor scoops the water and lays her hand on Marilee's forehead, she is startled, offended. She begins to cry again as the water drips onto her bubble dress.

Her eyes lock on to mine and they are filled with betrayal: "My dress! My dress is all wet!"

I kiss her and whisper, "It will dry, sweetie. It will dry."

In return, she wails.

When it is all over, we are supposed to walk up and down the aisle of the church so the children can be received by the community, but I march straight out the door to try to help Marilee calm down.

It is a disastrous and beautiful occasion and I have no idea what it means to them or how it will work out. But I am grateful.

That night, Peter decides to build a fire outside so we can introduce our children to s'mores. Marilee's eyes get wide, and she says, with apparent delight, "Mom, the graham crackers and marshmallows are going to go in my heart with Jesus!"

I don't tell her that she has a few things to learn about both anatomy and theology. We gather together around that fire, and amidst the roasting and the assembling and the eating, each child comes over for some time on my lap. The sky is black. We huddle together and consume the sticky sweetness.

I think back to William, cuddled next to me that morning in church when a guest musician offered a solo. It happened to be the song Penny used to ask for every night before bed—"He Knows My Name." William sat up straight, eager to participate. He sang loud and clear, the only member of the congregation to join in. He knew every word. *Before even time began, my life was in his hand.*

I can argue myself in circles about what the ceremony meant this morning. I know it isn't a magic incantation. I know we aren't putting God on the hook for Marilee's and William's eternal salvation. I know they may well walk away from the creeds and the hymns and the faith altogether when they get older. But I also know that something happened this morning, something that affirms the promise that God's hand is on my children's lives, keeping them close even when they seem far away. The theological back and forth gets me nowhere. But the reminder of God's promises quiets my soul. A gentle encouragement to trust. This Christian life of ours is messy and mysterious and beautiful. Like water, running down and spilling over.

marriage

Marriage is a gift God gives the church. He does not simply give it to the married people of the church, but to the whole church, just as marriage is designed not only for the benefit of the married couple. It is designed to tell a story to the entire church, a story about God's own love and fidelity to us.

—LAUREN F. WINNER, *REAL SEX*

"Mom, can you sing the when-you-get-married song?"

Penny is supposed to be getting dressed for school. Instead, she gazes up at me, her hands clasped together as if she is carrying a bouquet. She is wearing pink-footed pajamas and a look of starry-eyed wonder.

"Sweetie, I'm not sure what song you mean," I say. "It's time to get dressed."

"No, you know. About when you get married. Walking down the aisle? Come on, Mom."

"Kiddo, I really don't know. There are lots of songs for when you get married. And you're going to be late for school."

She sighs, and the wonder leaves her face. She starts to unzip her pajamas but stops abruptly. "The 'take my hand' song, Mom!"

I remember. I think about it for a minute, and then I start to sing.

Take my hand, and take my whole life too ...

She nods dreamily. We proceed through the morning routine. She brushes her teeth and puts on pink polka-dotted leggings, a gray skirt, and a cream-colored top. I open the curtains and help make her bed. I wipe Marilee's nose and clasp William's buttons. But this morning, unlike most, I sing.

I interrupt my singing to ask, "Did you all know I was in a singing group in high school? We used to sing this song."

They shake their heads. "Sing more, Momma. Sing more."

Wise men say only fools rush in, but I can't help falling in love with you ...

"And do you know what? Twenty years ago exactly on this day, your dad became my boyfriend."

William raises his eyebrows and looks like he is suppressing a smile. Penny sighs again, but this time it is a sigh of contentment instead of exasperation. Then she looks stern. "Mom. You need to fall in love with Dad all over again."

I shake my head, surprised by how suddenly my eyes feel prickly with gratitude. "No I don't, sweetie. I've been in love with him ever since."

* * *

We were an unlikely couple. We met when we were sixteen, one Saturday night when we were both at the same boarding school. I had never dated anyone before, whereas Peter had a reputation for always having a new girl on his arm. I graduated with the dubious distinction of "class Bible beater." He, "class flirt." But on the night we met, we talked for over an hour about friendship and God. Then he left a note in my mailbox, and he walked me back to my dorm one night, and then another, and then he kissed me, which was our community's way of signaling an official relationship. We were together.

I glossed over some of the harder times when I told Penny I've been in love with Peter ever since. The time I found out he kissed another girl at a senior party. The four years of being five hours apart from each other in college. The summer I wanted to have my own turn at rebellion and kiss other boys. The way I felt for months after I asked him to forgive me—as I wondered if the romance would ever return. And I didn't tell her that for us, having children has been the biggest test of our love for each other, the biggest crucible for those vows we pronounced so many years ago.

I didn't tell her that falling in love over and over again takes hard work.

For the first few years after we said *I do*, I told people we had an easy marriage. We didn't fight much, and even when conflicts did arise, we learned how to communicate our frustrations and concerns with each other. One night, for instance, I smiled sweetly, with my head cocked to the side, and asked, "Are you planning to take out the trash sometime soon or should I do it?" I could tell from his grimace and silence as he complied with my request that I had done something wrong. Later, he told me he would have preferred to have me swear at him while pointing to the garbage can. At least then he would know where things stood.

I had been raised in a household that avoided conflict at all costs. Peter had grown up expressing any and all emotion in a manner that usually involved yelling. The biggest struggle of our early years of marriage came as he tried to stay calm while expressing frustration and I tried to tell him how I felt without apology. We learned that a raised voice tended to render me useless, melted into a puddle underneath the dining room table. We learned that a passive-aggressive comment from me sparked a blaze of anger in him.

Even so, sustained conflict was rare. We worked together for a parachurch ministry for three years, sharing an office and almost all our meals. We made friends together. We joined a church together. We decided on a future together when he wanted to pursue teaching in a boarding school and I wanted to go to seminary. We went for walks and threw parties and cared for his mother when she was sick. And the love seemed easy.

Then we had Penny and William and Marilee, and even though I loved watching Peter become a father, learning whole new parts of him, we also began to feel protective of our time. We bargained about the early morning hours—whether they would be used for sleep or prayer or exercise. We handed off our children to give the other the chance to have coffee with a friend, take a walk, check email, play tennis. The love we had once reserved exclusively for each other needed to grow, needed to bleed out into a larger circle. And love now included waking up in the middle of the night for a child's trip to the potty, negotiations over which one of us would stay home on a snow day and who would take responsibility for swimming lessons and ballet class and learning to catch.

Time became our most precious commodity, and we guarded it jealously.

Even before we had children, I had requested a weekly date night. It started when Peter became the head of a dorm and we moved into an apartment in a house of thirty boys. I realized there would always be unexpected knocks on the door and phone calls and things to do around the house that would distract us from sitting across a table from one another without interruptions or agendas. Peter received a stipend for running the dorm, and I asked that the stipend go toward a dinner out, every week. So every week on Thursday afternoons I took a shower and blew my hair dry. I put on eye makeup and jewelry. I changed my clogs for shoes with a heel. And we went out to dinner.

We kept it up after the kids were born. It seemed romantic at first, but eventually I realized that going out to dinner every week was hard work. It cost a lot, both in time and money. Most weeks it was enjoyable—I often kept a list of thoughts I wanted to share and questions I wanted to ask. I cherished the feeling of wholeness that came from sitting across from Peter and listening to him talk about his day, offering the silly and profound details of my own.

We learned that we liked Indian food and that we didn't mind eating at a bar when a restaurant was full. We often strolled around campus after dinner, and those nights served as a magical break from the relentlessness of the regular routine. But they also forced us to face each other when we were hurt or angry. They forced us to look each other in the eye and talk about it when I felt like he didn't care about my career and when he felt like I was so protective of time alone that I neglected our family.

Time remained a precious commodity, and we gave it to each other week after week after week. And even during the weeks that brought tears and worry and hopelessness, my conviction remained. We were always in the process of loving each other, of falling in love all over again.

* * *

I walk Penny to the bus stop, and she asks me to sing some more. But then she cuts me off. "Mom, tell me the story about when you got married."

As we walk, leaves crunch underfoot. The air is crisp. The cedar waxwings landed in a tree in our front yard the day before, but already they have flown away. It all brings me back to walking through newly fallen leaves with Peter on a fall afternoon two decades earlier, wondering whether this high school romance could possibly last forever. Now I am walking down the road with my daughter, just one of the many unexpected gifts from that initial and unexpected falling-in-love so many years ago.

Penny tugs on my hand. "Mom! When you got married?"

"Yes. Right. Well, it was a June day, so the air felt different than today, but the sky was blue like right now. I went to the church and your Pop Pop walked me down the aisle—"

"I know you were in your wedding gown."

"Yes, that's right. In my wedding gown. And your dad was standing at the front of the church waiting for me."

"Was he looking at you?"

"Yes. He was wearing his glasses, and he was looking right at me and smiling and trying not to cry. Then we stood at the front of the church with the minister. And we promised we would love each other and take care of each other forever. And he gave me this ring—" I hold out my hand to show the slim gold band— "and then we were married."

"And he kissed you!"

"And he kissed me. Then we walked out of the church and we had a big party because we were so happy to be married."

We arrive at the bus stop. Penny lets go of my hand and runs to greet her friends.

I walk home alone, scuffing my clogs against the pavement, breathing deeply with gratitude for the reminder of the gifts our life together has brought so far. I think back to those vows and what it has meant to live them out. We have wounded each other. We have helped one another heal. We have taken care of each other in sickness and in health, through his mother's illness, through the early days of Penny's diagnosis, through harrowing sleepless nights with William, through the chaos of adding Marilee to our family, through moves and master's degrees and career changes, through petty betrayals and the slog of reconciliation.

But one thing has stayed the same: I am still in love with that boy. It is a feeling that has now been grounded in the real stuff of pain and death and suffering and beauty and joy and healing, but the lightness, the giddiness, the excitement, the wonder—that he counts me as belonging to him and he to me—the wonder remains.

Twenty years later, I am still glad this fool rushed in.

grace

All human nature vigorously resists grace because grace changes us and the change is painful.

—FLANNERY O'CONNOR, *THE HABIT OF BEING*

I set my alarm for 6:00 a.m. so I can make a cup of tea and sit in our dining room and read and pray before the house awakens. We have finally transitioned into a time when all three children usually sleep through the night. We are starting to feel settled. I am starting to regain a rhythm to my days. This morning, I begin my prayer requests by writing, *For help paying attention to Marilee. I worry that she gets less of us than she deserves.*

Approximately two minutes later, I hear crying from upstairs. Two-year-old Marilee is awake, an hour earlier than usual.

My first response is irritation. She's interrupting my contemplative moment! She's getting in the way of my plan!

And then I laugh out loud. She is also an answer to prayer.

A few days later, Marilee has a fever and is rubbing her right ear. So I take her to the doctor and discover she has a double ear infection, which may, come to think of it, have been what woke her up so early. She takes antibiotics for ten days. Two weeks pass, and then she has a high fever. I take her back in.

Double ear infection still present. Another round of antibiotics, this time with a follow-up appointment. At that checkup, both ears are still infected, so our pediatrician sends us to a specialist forty-five minutes away.

During the car ride to the specialist, we sing and talk about her friends at school and she asks me questions like, "When I gonna get oldah, Mommy? When I gonna dwive a cawah?"

We go to the mall and I take her to lunch at Panera.

The specialist prescribes round three of antibiotics and suggests we return in two weeks.

And as I suppress a sigh at the thought of three more hours to get to the doctor and home again, I remember that prayer from months earlier. I remember how often I have bypassed opportunities to be alone with Marilee. I've sent her to extra hours of school when I've had too much work to do. I've gotten together with friends and their children on mornings when she and I could have been alone together. I've done housework and parked her in front of an iPad.

But these Friday morning trips to the doctor have been just the two of us. Time to hold hands and listen to her count to ten. Time to let her push the button on the elevator without competing with her older siblings. Time to wrangle her into her car seat, even though she desperately wants to be four years old and sit on a booster like her brother. Time to blow kisses. Time to get to know my daughter.

Two weeks later, we come back and the infection is gone but there is still fluid in her ears, which leads to a third visit to the specialist two weeks after that, at which point Marilee is finally pronounced healed.

I never thought I'd find myself grateful for a lingering double ear infection and hours and hours of related doctor's appointments. I never thought I'd consider a double ear infection an answer to prayer.

When she wakes up from a nap at the end of these ten weeks, I say, "I love you Marilee."

She says, "Love me so much?"

"So much," I say.

"This so much?" she asks, arms outstretched.

I love you even more than that.

* * *

A few nights later, Penny lies in bed framed by pink. Pink polka-dotted pillow. Pink cupcake pajamas. A round pink face that looks dreamy and content as I sing.

"Amazing grace—" I begin.

But she puts out her hand. "Mom, wait. Why don't you sing amazing Penny?"

I stifle a laugh and say, "Why would I do that, sweetheart?"

She says, "You know. Amazing Grace, amazing Penny. Like Grace from school."

This time I laugh out loud. "Oh sweetie, I see. It's not a song about Grace from school. It's a song about God's grace, which means God's love and forgiveness for us."

"Oh!" she replies, as if I have explained something that had been confusing for a long time.

She is asleep before I finish singing, but I sit with her a few minutes longer, just thinking about her comment. *Amazing Penny.* And I think about the ways in which all three of our children are a means of grace in my life. Penny, the one who teaches me by being so different from me. Showing me patience, and gratitude, and what it looks like to work hard without worrying about being the best. Teaching me how to pray, how to see beauty, how to love.

William, who teaches me by being so similar to me. I think back to his dedication as an infant in our church in Princeton, when the pastor happened to pick a verse from 2 Timothy: "You then, my son, be strong in the grace that is in Christ Jesus." Our pastor didn't know that the pediatrician had already expressed neurological concerns about William's strength—his muscles were so tight I had trouble getting him into his clothes as an infant. The strength turned out simply to be high muscle tone and required no medical intervention. But I have prayed these words for William, my strong son, ever since. That William might be strong in grace, strong in caring for others, strong in love. And that his mother would be strong right there with him. Strong in grace. Learning how to laugh, how to fail, how to let go, how to love.

Then there is Marilee, so well named with her effervescent smile, so ready to jump into the fray of our family, so eager to bring happiness to everyone around her. Marilee, the one I could easily miss in the midst of our busyness and noise. Marilee, the one God gives back to me by way of a double ear infection and laughter and kisses and car rides. Teaching me how to live with joy, with gratitude, with grace.

* * *

Amazing Penny.
Amazing William.
Amazing Marilee.
Amazing grace, how sweet the sound.

acknowledgments

This book is a story of growth. Not only the growth of our family, but also the growth that has happened—that is happening— within me as I learn to receive what my children offer. As I relate within these pages, my kids have helped me to learn more about gratitude and dependency. Writing books has helped me to learn these things too. And so I come to the end of this book feeling very grateful and also very aware of how impossible it would have been to write without the support and encouragement of a host of others.

On the day I received confirmation from Zondervan that they wanted to publish this book, we happened to be having dinner as a family outside. Marilee was still too young to get what was going on, but Penny and William suggested we "cheers" the occasion. They clinked their plastic cups of milk against my Diet Coke. Over the course of the year that I wrote *Small Talk*, I often reminded them at dinner of some of our escapades together. The story about our failed trip to the grocery store has become an epic journey in their minds. The fact that William and I used to fight all the time and now we are friends has become a sweet reminder of the gifts of growing up. Through it all, I have felt my gratitude for our family grow and grow. Marilee, William,

Penny—thank you for teaching me so much and for loving me so well. And Peter, without you there would be no story to tell. You were the first one to remind me of the healing that comes through laughter. Thank you.

On a more professional note, my agent Chris Park once again deserves more credit than she will ever receive—for conceiving of this book and rerouting me when I was stubbornly insisting on another direction altogether, for coming up with the title, and for championing my work every step of the way. I could also not be more thankful for the team at Zondervan—Sandy, Elisa, Londa, and Dirk in particular—and for their shared vision and wisdom in bringing this project to completion.

Some of the anecdotes and thoughts contained within these pages appeared in more rudimentary form in a variety of publications before they made their way into this manuscript. I am grateful to Katelyn Beaty at *Christianity Today* and Lisa Belkin, formerly at *Motherlode* and at *The Huffington Post*, for their encouragement in writing about our family and how our children have pushed me to grow up.

I should also note that the epigraphs for each chapter come from books that have been particularly meaningful to me. I recommend them all as a way to further explore the topics I only begin to address here.

Finally, to Ellen and Jen, who read early drafts and encouraged me to keep going, and to Patricia, who critiqued and encouraged and pushed me further and further toward grace— thank you.

questions for reflection and discussion

These questions are intended to help you individually or in a group setting consider the themes of *Small Talk* in relation to your own story. This guide is designed for a one-time gathering. For chapter-by-chapter questions to be used over the course of several small group sessions or for personal use, please go to www.amyjuliabecker.com.

1. What did you find most helpful about *Small Talk*?

2. Why do you think children offer such insights about grand topics like death, beauty, and faith?

3. In "Birth," Amy Julia writes, "Just as physical birth is messy and complicated, being born spiritually is not a neat and tidy transformation. It is an ongoing story of neediness and growth and trust." How do you see this theme carried throughout the book? Have you experienced anything similar in your own life?

4. In what ways does having children change people?

5. Why do you think parenting brings such a mix of positive and negative emotions?

6. Amy Julia often reflects back on things she learned or wishes she had learned in her own childhood. What is one thing you wish you had learned in childhood that you have learned as an adult?

7. In "Sin," Amy Julia writes, "Limitations ... lead to love." How does Amy Julia grow in love as a result of her limitations? Have you seen a similar pattern in your own life? In what ways do your failures lead to stronger relationships?

8. Several chapters — "Christmas," "Beauty," and "Easter" in particular — address the connection between the material world and the spiritual world. Why is the material world important? How does it connect to the spiritual?

9. Songs are an important part of Amy Julia's faith and family. What role has music played in your personal growth?

10. Over the course of the book, Amy Julia teaches her children to be more independent. At the same time, she is growing in her dependence on God and others. How do maturity, independence, and dependence work together?

11. In what ways, if any, have you become more like a child over the years of adulthood? How does becoming childlike help us grow up?

12. Pick one chapter epigraph (quote at the beginning of the chapter) that particularly resonated with you. What did you find meaningful about it?

13. What do the part titles — "Holding On," "Letting Go," "Growing Up" — have to do with faith? What do they have to do with parenting?

14. In the opening epigraph to the book (from Marilynne Robinson's *Gilead*), as well as in "Beginning" (the introduction) and "Grace" (the final chapter), Amy Julia speaks of her children as God's grace to her. What do you think it looks like to be God's grace to someone?

15. Amy Julia responds to her children's questions throughout the book. What questions remain for her and for you?

notes

Birth

Page 21: *born again*: John 3:3.

Rest

Page 48: *"For in six days the Lord ..."*: Exodus 20:11.
Page 49: *"Remember that you were slaves ..."*: Deuteronomy 5:15.
Page 52: *"He makes me lie down ..."*: Psalm 23:2.

Jesus

Page 65: *look into her eyes and call her, "Daughter"*: Luke 8:48.
Page 67: *"the image of the invisible ..."*: Colossians 1:15.
Page 67: *"God with us"*: Matthew 1:23.

Beauty

Page 72: *"Your body is a temple ..."*: 1 Corinthians 3:16.
Page 73: *"Man looks at the outward ..."*: 1 Samuel 16:7.
Page 73: *"Your beauty should not come ..."*: 1 Peter 3:3–4.

Gratitude

Page 88: *"One of them, when he ..."*: Luke 17:15–16.
Page 90: *"whatever is right"*: Matthew 20:4.
Page 90: *"Why have you been standing ..."*: Matthew 20:6–7.
Page 91: *"You have made them equal ..."*: Matthew 20:12.
Page 91: *"Are you envious because I am ..."*: Matthew 20:15.
Page 91: *"So the last will be ..."*: Matthew 20:16.

Sin

Page 95: *"all have sinned and fall ..."*: Romans 3:23.

Waiting

Page 105: *"learned the secret of ..."*: Philippians 4:12.

Easter

Page 112: *He claimed that the reason ...*: Acts 2:24–36.
Page 112: *"If Christ has not been ..."*: 1 Corinthians 15:14.
Page 113: *"we are of all people ..."*: 1 Corinthians 15:19.

God

Page 126: *When Jesus teaches his disciples*: Matthew 6:9.
Page 128: *"When I consider your heavens ..."*: Psalm 8:3–4.

Happiness

Page 140: *the Beatitudes*: Matthew 5:1–12.

Love

Page 155: *"God is love"*: 1 John 4:8.
Page 157: *"Be imitators of God ..."*: Ephesians 5:1–2.

Kindness

Page 179: *"I am the Lord, your God ..."*: Isaiah 41:13.

Forgiveness

Page 185: *"Son, your sins are forgiven"*: Mark 2:5.

Friendship

Page 207: *instead, he called them friends*: John 15:15.

Grace

Page 230: *"You then, my son, be strong ..."*: 2 Timothy 2:1.